THE FIRST AND SECOND
EPISTLES OF PETER

NEW TESTAMENT FOR SPIRITUAL READING

VOLUME 22

Edited by

John L. McKenzie, S.J.

THE FIRST EPISTLE
OF PETER

BENEDIKT SCHWANK

THE SECOND EPISTLE
OF PETER

ALOIS STÖGER

CROSSROAD · NEW YORK

1981
The Crossroad Publishing Company
575 Lexington Avenue, New York, NY 10022

Originally published as *Der erste Brief des Apostels Petrus*
and *Der zweite Brief des Apostels Petrus*
© 1963, 1966 by Patmos-Verlag
from the series *Geistliche Schriftlesung*
edited by Wolfgang Trilling
with Karl Hermann Schelke and Heinz Schürmann

English translation © 1969 by Burns & Oates, Limited, London
The First Epistle of Peter was translated by Walter Kruppa
The Second Epistle of Peter was translated by W. Jerman

Library of Congress Catalog Card Number: 81-68175
ISBN: 0-8245-0131-4

PREFACE

The first epistle of Peter can be attributed with tradition to Peter, as long as one admits that Silvanus had an important part in its composition; it is highly improbable that Peter could write as good Greek as we have in the first epistle. For reasons which modern scholars find convincing the second epistle cannot be the work of Peter, but must be some years later than the death of Peter. The differences in style and vocabulary, as well as the development of doctrine in the epistle, are decisive. The two epistles are included among the Catholic or General Epistles because they are not addressed to any particular church. The first epistle is addressed to churches in some regions of Asia Minor, and the second epistle is addressed to no one. They are homilies or tracts rather than epistles.

The first epistle has a primarily moral interest; this it shares with many passages of the Pauline epistles and with the epistle of James. The moral interest is viewed under a somewhat new light; the exhortations are addressed to Christians who are suffering persecution or are threatened by persecution. It has been noticed that there was no general persecution during the life of Peter, and the language of the epistle really does not permit one to affirm that a general persecution is implied. Some interpreters have suggested that the writer is not thinking of persecution in the usual sense of the word, but only of the petty persecution which the Christian often experiences from his unbelieving neighbors and acquaintances.

Persecution is one of the two extremes which threaten the

moral integrity of the Christian; the other extreme is prosperity.
Both extremes are mentioned in the New Testament, and the
allusions to persecution very probably arise from real persecution,
either threats to life or the petty persecution of ordinary experience. The reality of the threat of petty persecution should
not be minimized; it is much more a part of the normal Christian experience than attacks on life, limb and property, and
because it can be sustained over a long period of time it may
wear down resistance more surely than more serious persecution. The threat to life is the kind of moral crisis which can
and does elicit a response of unexpected strength; it is recognized as a crisis, and it is possible that a single decision will
resolve the crisis. No single decision resolves the crisis of constant petty persecution, the harassment of dislike, of discrimin-
atory treatment, of loss of esteem and reputation, of condemnation to a permanent low grade in one's community. Were
persecution really planned by some superior intelligence, nothing but petty persecution would be employed. Tertullian said
in Roman times that the blood of martyrs is the seed of Christians.

The first epistle presents Jesus Christ as an example of the
Christian life. In spite of the long tradition of " the imitation
of Christ " in Christian spirituality, this theme is very rare in
the New Testament. The Christian is not urged to imitate Jesus
in the working of miracles or in his authoritative proclamations.
Where Jesus is proposed as a model, as he is in the first epistle
of Peter, the model is defined in severely limited terms. One
does not become an authentic Christian by adopting the dress
and manner of life of a Palestinian peasant of the first century;
this was recognized even in the first century. The imitation of
Jesus, if the phrase must be used, is something much more

subtle which must be within the reach of all Christians, whatever their country, their culture, their date or their station in
life.

The author of the first epistle presents Jesus as an example
of bearing suffering. The first feature of Christian suffering is
that it be innocent; one who receives deserved punishment for
wrongdoing is not experiencing Christian suffering. The statement needs expansion; for the repentant wrongdoer may turn
his punishment into Christian suffering. What the author has
in mind is suffering for one's faith, which is surely innocent if
no other factors are involved. It is rather surprising that so
many other factors have so often been involved. Insistence on
innocent suffering is not at all a superfluous element in the
homily of First Peter; in fact the Christian cannot easily
assume that he is an innocent victim even if he is persecuted
for his faith.

The second feature of Christian suffering is that the Christian does not return evil for evil, either by word or by deed.
Even less than in the first feature can the Christian assume that
he suffers without returning evil. We have called the imitation
of Jesus subtle. Subtlety in this area consists in recognizing the
excuses for defense or even for aggressive counteraction for what
they are. One resists suffering because the good of the church
must be defended, the good of the church meaning perhaps the
property of the church or the dignity of its officers. One may
best defend the church by removing those who persecute it or
might persecute it. One may defend the church by bolstering
the church with so much political and economic power that it is
above all attack. One cannot see the imitation of Jesus in any
of these tactics.

The second epistle of Peter has a single concern, and that is eschatology. The student of the New Testament soon learns that the Second Coming was one of the most active theological questions in the apostolic church. Some documents exhibit a clear and unsophisticated expectation that the Second Coming was only a few years away. Other documents, of which Second Peter is one, show a resignation to the fact that the Second Coming is indefinitely deferred. " Resignation " would not be felt had it not been felt that the Second Coming was in some way demanded as a vindication of God's power and will to save. The delay of the Second Coming therefore demanded some rationalization. Second Peter is one such rationalization.

The Christians must understand that God's mysterious tolerance of evil is not due to his inability to cope with evil. The temptation to this type of disbelief is common enough to be mentioned in numerous biblical passages in both Testaments. They must await God's judgment, assured that the longer it is delayed the more terrible it will be. Second Peter appeals, actually in a rather restrained way, to the apocalyptic imagery which is found in some Old Testament books, a few other New Testament passages, and in the apocryphal books of Judaism. The imagery of these books should be recognized as imagery, not as actual and literal predictions of future events. The judgments of God are difficult to recognize and even more difficult to describe. No description, even in biblical books, attains the reality. Some are so repelled by the imagery that they lose faith in the judgment. Others are so fascinated by the imagery that they allow their own vindictiveness to cloud their vision of God's love and mercy. The apocalyptic visions of judgment must be retained as a part of the biblical revelation of God; they should neither be entirely abandoned nor made the key passages of the Bible.   JOHN L. McKENZIE, S.J.

The First Epistle
of Peter

INTRODUCTION

Grace and the Cross

In the oldest pastoral letter (cf. 5 : 2–4; 2 : 25) in the history of the church, Peter in collaboration with Silvanus concludes by saying that he has written, " exhorting and declaring," to assure the recipients that, in spite of their afflictions, they are on the right path and that they truly stand in the grace of God (5 : 12). What does this standing in the grace of God mean?

Peter speaks of it in several places. Seen with the eyes of faith a slave, for instance, stands in the grace of God, who endures undeserved vexations without hate (2 : 19), who does good, has to suffer as a result, and unerringly goes his way in spite of it (2 : 20). This grace, foretold by the prophets of the old covenant (1 : 10), and representing the final aim of the Christian life (1 : 13; 3 : 7; 5 : 10), often means suffering in this earthly life: suffering which is permitted by God—indeed, which is valuable in his sight (3 : 14). To suffer in accordance with God's will means to stand in the grace of God.

The basis of this concept of grace is that man in his suffering becomes like the crossbearing Lord, like Jesus " who, when he was reviled, did not revile, when he suffered did not threaten " (2 : 23), who has suffered before us to give us " an example " (2 : 21) which we could imitate and which enables us " to follow in his footsteps " (2 : 21). Christ's way of the cross, rich in grace, raised him to the right hand of the Father (3 : 18–22). Therefore, Peter exhorts us to rejoice whenever we partake in the suffering of Christ since in this way we shall also exultingly partake in the revelation of eternal glory (4:13).

The image of standing in grace is the key to the understanding of this letter. Nevertheless it is but one of many images all of which aim at consoling and exhorting Christians tried by suffering.

The exhortation to follow Christ, which permeates this letter, belongs to the matrix of the young church's instruction. There is hardly a piece of New Testament scripture which so immediately reflects the spirit of the young community than the first letter of Peter. In this letter, containing only 105 verses, all the essential points of the theological thought of the young church are recognizable. In a meditative reading of this letter we are again and again confronted with those thoughts which we are accustomed to find in the Lord's Prayer and in the Apostles' Creed, that is to say, with the oldest building stones of Christian theology.

It would be incorrect to imagine Peter's authorship of this letter as in any way comparable with that of a private letter in the modern sense. The history of its composition can be better compared with that of a modern papal encyclical. It is a communal work, behind which, nonetheless, the living authority of Peter stands.

Three collaborators can be clearly discerned. To begin with there is the evangelist Mark, called the " son " of Peter in 5:13. Church tradition tells us that he was active in Rome as Peter's interpreter and catechist. His gospel, however, shows that the polished form, the skillful choice of Greek words and the sometimes rhythmic flow of this letter could not have originated from him.

A more important collaborator than Mark, however, seems

to have been Silvanus. He is also expressly mentioned in the final greeting of the letter (5:12). Silvanus was a prominent figure in the young church, and enjoyed great respect in the Jewish-Christian community of Jerusalem (Acts 15:22). Moreover, as a Roman citizen (Acts 16:25, 35-39) he would have benefited from a thorough education. He had been for many years the companion of the apostle Peter (Acts 18:5; 1 and 2 Thess. 1) and was regarded in the heathen-Christian communities as a " prophet " who had the gift of " exhorting and strengthening " (Acts 15:32).

The third and most important collaborator is also mentioned in the final greeting: the community in Rome, the " sister-church in Babylon " (5:13). In this community, in the only city of more than a million inhabitants then known to have existed, there was a constant coming and going of Christians from all parts of the Mediterranean. It had already become the pulsing heart of the entire church.

In spite of the obvious collaboration of others, the spirit and the living personality of the *kephas* himself shines through. His wholly personal constancy in faith matured by humility, his communion with Christ, his love for the cross, his pastoral concern and the awareness of his responsibility as chief " presbyter " (5:1-5) inspire the entire epistle.

The recipients are the baptized Christians of the numerous communities of the provinces of Asia Minor referred to in 1:2, who are exhorted in view of their dignity as baptized persons. There are, moreover, specific exhortations for definite classes, that is, for household servants (2:18-25), for housewives (3:1-6), for husbands (3:7), and for clerics (5:1-5). There are manifold references to a former " vain manner of life " (1:18), to a time of " ignorance " in which they formerly lived (1:14), to the worship of idols and the dissipation of their former life (4:3).

Yet they are already well acquainted with the Old Testament
(1:16; 2:9; 3:6).

The communities, therefore, consist mainly of former heathens
who before their conversion to Christianity had either already
been circumcised, or at least had, as God-fearing people, come
into contact with Judaic monotheism and with the scriptures in
the Greek translation of the Septuagint. Such adult, mature, and
tried Christians, living in the midst of the Babylonian turmoil,
Peter primarily has in mind when he addresses them as chosen
ones and strangers in the diaspora (1:1).

The letter was brought by Silvanus from Rome to Asia Minor
about the year 64, that is on the eve of the Christian persecution
under Nero. Blood has not yet flowed, but severe persecutions
are threateningly near. One reckons with official interrogation
(3:15), and private vexations and slanders (2:12; 3:16). The
faith of the recipients is beginning to be tested as gold in a
furnace (1:7; 4:12). In terrifying premonition Peter paints the
threatening danger of the Anti-Christ in the image of a roaring
lion who goes about seeking whom he could lead astray into
infidelity (5:8).

Thus it happens that this encouraging pastoral letter, written
in the sixties of the first century to Christians tried by suffering,
has become the letter of consolation of the persecuted church of
all centuries. Again and again, in last letters from dungeons
and prisons one comes upon words taken, precisely, from this
letter. Its magnificent, optimistic view of world history based on
faith, which reduces earthly trials to " a little while " of time
(1:6; 5:10), has given consolation and strength in the most
difficult times. Thus this letter of the representative of Christ has
become *the* letter of martyrs: martyrs for their faith in Christ
(1:8), for their hope in eternal life (3:15), and for their fidelity
to the ecclesial community.

OUTLINE

The Opening of the Letter (1 : 1–2)

THE ADDRESS (1 : 1–2)
  I. The sender (1 : 1a)
 II. The recipients (1 : 1b–2a)
III. The greeting (1 : 2b)

The Body of the Letter (1 : 3—5 : 11)

THE GREATNESS OF THE CHRISTIAN CALLING (1 : 3—2 : 10)
  I. Thanksgiving for the call (1 : 3–12)
    1. Thanksgiving to the Father (1 : 3–5)
    2. Thanksgiving for salvation in Christ (1 : 6–9)
    3. Thanksgiving for the help of the Holy Spirit (1 : 10–12)
 II. Christian life—the true exodus of Israel (1 : 13—2 : 10)
    1. Gird yourselves hopefully (1 : 13)
    2. Become holy (1 : 14–16)
    3. Be willing to obey (1 : 17–21)
    4. Love one another (1 : 22–25)
    5. Long for the word of God like thirsty infants (2 : 1–3)
    6. Let yourselves be built (2 : 4–6)
    7. Summing up: God's holy people (2 : 7–10)

THE RESPONSIBILITIES OF THOSE CALLED (2 : 11—4 : 11)
  I. General and basic counsels (2 : 11–12)
    1. Personal abstentions (2 : 11)
    2. An exemplary way of life (2 : 12)

THE OPENING OF THE LETTER
(1:1-2)

THE ADDRESS (1:1-2)

Excepting the words of the Lord himself which are handed down to us in the gospels, no text of the New Testament addresses us with such authority as the opening of this letter.

The Sender (1:1a)

¹ᵃPeter, an apostle of Jesus Christ, . . .

Petrus means here exactly what originally the Aramaic word, which Christ gave to Simon as a new surname, expressed: *kepha, the rock.* Christ wished to indicate that Simon, in accordance with God's plan of salvation, was to partake in the divine permanence and insuperability. In the old covenant Yahweh is often called the " rock " of Israel and in the New Testament Christ is the rock (1 Cor. 10:4). This name, which expresses a divine characteristic, was given to a weak human being. Only in faith can man participate in the permanence of God. Hence the father of our faith, Abraham, was called the rock by the prophet Isaiah (cf. Is. 51:1f.). He was predestined by God as the foundation of his chosen people. For the new and true Israel, Kephas takes his place.

Peter calls himself an apostle. " Apostle " was at this time a fixed concept. The idea of ambassador was here secondary to that of plenipotentiary, or representative. Then, of course, the decisive question was whose apostle someone was. In the second letter to

3

the Corinthians we hear of the " apostle of the communities " (8 : 23). Here, however, we hear of the " apostle of Jesus Christ." An incredible tension lies in these first words: Peter, who through faith participates in the permanence of God and forms the rock-foundation of the church, begins on behalf of Jesus Christ and as his plenipotentiary to exhort and to console.

The Recipients (1 : 1b–2a)

1b. . . . *to the exiles of the dispersion in Pontus, Galatia, Cappadocia, Asia, and Bithynia, chosen . . .*

Addressed are *chosen people* who are, at the same time, strangers living in diaspora, or dispersion. The first Christians knew that it belongs to the essence of being Christian to be chosen, to be called—in the free eternal choice of God's grace, to be undeservedly preferred. This is the first address, the basis of Christian life. He who was called became a stranger in his environment. A calling to sanctity and renunciation belong together. At the same time these two words illumine something that is fundamental to the Christian in relation to his non-Christian environment. As did once the Israel of the flesh so does the true Israel, the church, live in exile and diaspora far away from its eternal home. In its early days the exercise of the Christian religion was illegal in the Roman state. The early Christians are here addressed as " chosen strangers," " chosen ones," and " strangers," to let it be known that the sender is aware of their many sufferings but also to indicate his positive judgment of such trials.

The Christians are chosen ones and strangers of the " diaspora," literally of the dispersion. They are this not only because they are dispersed geographically in Asia Minor but also because the spiritual situation of all Christians corresponds to that of the Jewish people in the Babylonian captivity: far from the mother country, from the heavenly Jerusalem. But in captivity Israel was at the same time dispersed among the peoples. Hence "dispersion" has a positive meaning. In spite of the separateness due to being "called apart," there is a task to be performed in the unbelieving world surrounding those of the diaspora: by a God-fearing life and through good works, those who are chosen are to be witnesses to the invisible God.

²ᵃ. . . *and destined by God the Father and sanctified by the Spirit for obedience to Jesus Christ and for sprinkling with his blood:*

Before the actual greeting and prayer for peace is uttered, Peter sets the stage by telling us that our situation has been brought about by the saving action of the triune God. The *Father* stands at the head. We have been called and chosen in baptism by the eternal "foreknowledge," the providence of the Father, which is at the same time a loving effective predestination for eternal life. What is said of Christ with the same word (1 : 20) is said of each individual one of us: God's love has concerned itself with us from eternity.

Since the day of our baptism we were drawn into the progressive, powerful action of the holy and sanctifying *Spirit*. And in the degree to which we grow into this new reality the profane word becomes strange to us. By this "sanctification" from the Spirit, Christian life begins, and in the sanctifying power of this Spirit it is to be perfected in holiness.

In his statement concerning our relation to the *Son* of God Peter uses words which first of all remind us of the exodus of

Israel from Egypt, which is so often referred to in this letter. When the people of Israel had been chosen, through God's providence, and then, prefiguring baptism, gone through the Red Sea, and had begun their journey to the Holy Land, they promised obedience on Sinai to all the commandments of God. This covenant was sealed with the sprinkling of blood. The covenant prefigured the reconciliation that has occurred between us and the triune God through the death of Jesus Christ.

It was Jesus' "food and drink" to do the will of the Father (Jn. 4:34). We too are chosen for obedience, called to profess obedience, to listen to the call of the Father, to follow it as did Jesus. For the man who follows Christ, being attentive to God's will in everyday life means the confirmation and realization of his faith, his humility, and above all his childlike love.

The Greeting (1:2b)

2bMay grace and peace be multiplied to you.

This greeting and blessing of the first Christians, "grace and peace," is distinctly more meaningful than the greetings found in the opening of non-Christian letters of that time. The latter often began with a simple "greetings," "let you be greeted," or, perhaps, "good health."

Above all, grace is to increase, that is, the favor and condescension of God is to increase. May God's eternal, free will turn to us, that loving condescension, which has singled us out from eternity and has chosen us for sanctity, for obedience and for a new covenant sealed by the blood of the only Son. This favor of God will make us pleasing even to God. The word "grace" is

best understood as " pleasing to God." That is the gracious, con-
descending, self-giving goodness of God—and also the consequence of such giving, the becoming pleasing to God of a fav-
ored man. In the course of the letter there will often be mention
of things which are especially pleasing to God: above all innocent, freely accepted suffering (2:19f.) and humble submission
(5:5). Indeed, Peter sees in this theme the main concern of his
entire letter, grace, and sums it up with the words that Christians in their suffering and difficulties are on the right path, since
through them they stand in the grace, in the pleasure of God. It
is not seldom that the grace of God takes on the form of the
cross of Christ.

As in the greeting of the angel to the shepherds before the
walls of Bethlehem, just so did the wish and certainty of peace
belong to the greeting of the young church from the beginning.
This biblical freedom is not an undisturbed quietness. Peace
according to scripture reigns only where the God of peace is in
full control. Thus the liberation from the servility of sin becomes
a presupposition to this peace, which earthly powers could never
establish. Not until God has full power in our soul do we participate in Christ's victorious peace.

THE BODY OF THE LETTER
(1:3—5:11)

THE GREATNESS
OF THE CHRISTIAN CALLING (1:3—2:10)

After Peter has expressed in the greeting of the letter his wish for grace and peace, he reminds the recipients of the great mystery of rebirth. There is consolation and encouragement to be found in the fact that they are called to form God's holy people.

Thanksgiving for the Call (1:3-12)

Thanksgiving to the Father (1 : 3-5)

³Blessed be the God and Father of our Lord Jesus Christ! By his great mercy we have been born anew to a living hope through the resurrection of Jesus Christ from the dead . . .

In the first place there is homage to the Father, a grateful exclamation of joy: May he be " blessed," praised and glorified; which he " is " from eternity to eternity through his creation. The word " blessed " implies the Hebrew *baruch*. A " baruch " is for the Oriental someone to whom one pays homage on bended knee, blessing and glorifying him through word and deed. In later Judaism the title " the blessed One " actually became a divine name, the name of him whose praise and glorification is the meaning of creation and the end and highest honor of the human being.

The special standpoint from which God is here pronounced

11

blessed as the Father of our Lord Jesus Christ is his fatherhood towards us as well. He is our Father not only on the grounds of our natural conception in our mother's womb, which would have been impossible without his will, but even more so in that he has become the father of our new life, the cause of our new birth. He was plainly compelled to this life-giving act " by his great mercy." The word " mercy " here refers less to his sympathy with the miserable and poor as his intimate bond with humanity since the Garden of Eden.

Later we hear more clearly how this " new birth " is to be understood. " You have been born anew, not of perishable seed but of imperishable, through the living and abiding word of God " (1:23). Christians should remember the day when for the first time the message of the death and above all of the resurrection of Christ was brought to them, the day when first this heavenly seed fell into their hearts and began to grow. This new life with Christ based on faith achieved visible expression, commitment and external significance in baptism, the sacrament of rebirth.

This wonderful seed, which God has sown in our hearts, is Christian hope. Through the entire letter there sounds a basic note of hope. The hope in question here is not a pious wish, but a living reality, best compared with the mother's hope for a child which is carried in her womb. True Christian hope looks forward to the return of Christ and the kingdom of God, but in spite of this it will begin to live and to grow here; hoping, it participates in the need of the despairing; it wishes to contribute to the victory of goodness and truth already in this earthly everyday life insofar as this is possible. It is like the " kingdom of heaven " : it begins here already, although its final end resides outside earthly existence. Human hope was quickened by the resurrection of Christ, and Christian hope looks to the day of death as a mother awaits the pangs and joys of the birth of her first child.

⁴ . . . *and to an inheritance which is imperishable, undefiled, and unfading, kept in heaven for you . . .*

This new life as children of God was given to us in view of an *inheritance* which we are to receive. There must be something wonderful about an inheritance described by so many unusual adjectives. In the old covenant every tribe of Israel received by lot its inheritance in the promised land, its ground and soil. For us also there awaits at the end of our journey, of our life, a holy, transfigured " land " which we are to receive as a reward. When we imagine this " land " to be the bodies of resurrected persons then words like imperishable, undefiled, and unfading become more intelligible for what awaits us, for what is kept for us—not in a larder or trunk, but in the loving heart of God. Through imperishability the body will be like to God and free from all corruption of sin. Undefiled and without spot it will glisten pure as snow since no earthly stain will any longer adhere to it, and this gift of God will shine unfading in eternal youthful beauty.

⁵ . . . *who by God's power are guarded through faith for a salvation ready to be revealed in the last time.*

The danger of the Christian way of life lies in the thousand possibilities to err from the beaten track and never to reach the goal. Peter is aware of this anxiety of Christians. So he immediately adds to this vision of the glorious goal the consolation of God's assistance in the meantime. We are watched over, guarded by and in the might of God. The word " to guard," which is used here, is found in other places when there is talk of the protection and defense of a city. Not only the whole church of Christ, but also every community, every family, and every single soul is a city, a bulwark, whose walls the ungodly forces attack and assail always anew and often in ambush (cf. 2:11). But this city possesses a solid defense in the powerful protection of God, as it were its puissant battlements. The bond with God built on faith forms this impregnable solid battlement, which will guard us in the course of our lives.

But Peter does not stop at the thought of the threat on the way. Immediately the goal, the salvation, which God has prepared for us, comes into sight once more. This salvation is never merely the private affair of the individual. Christian salvation is always concerned with the perfection of the community in which the Christian resides, indeed, the perfection of the entire church. This salvation has already dawned upon us. In the future it will be completed and joyfully disclosed. Since our baptism we possess this salvation, still hidden and invisible to our neighbor. It needs only to grow and await the revelation : await that last day on which the veil shall be removed.

Thanksgiving for Salvation in Christ (1:6–9)

⁶In this you rejoice though now for a little while you may have to suffer various trials, ⁷so that the genuineness of your faith, more precious than gold which though perishable is tested by fire, may redound to praise and glory and honor at the revelation of Jesus Christ.

Christians can and should rejoice at this salvation (1:5), although this joy is yet darkened in this earthly life, and they still " suffer various trials." The persecution of Christians under Nero had not yet begun but early signs were at hand. Peter wants to say to the young Christian communities that they shall probably have to suffer, but their joy at salvation is so great that trials dull their happiness only a little. No mention is yet made of a bloody persecution of Christians, or of glorious martyrs; rather, the letter is concerned with the daily difficulties of Christians who faced heathen surroundings, at the place of work, even in the families—faced those who were annoyed and scandalized at people who took seriously humble obedience, sorrow at human sins, forgiveness of injustice, practice of chastity and voluntary deprivation. Personal insults, slanders, setbacks—these are the various trials which we often find so painful. The suffering that the Christian has to bear is in reality a purification, a smelting and tempering (cf. 4:12) of his true, genuine faith. We know that already in ancient times gold coins were put into circulation which in reality were only gilded. Because of the high weight of gold, lead was especially suitable for such mixtures. By heating, it soon became clear whether an inferior metal had been added to the so-called gold coin. Moreover, in the old covenant we often encounter the image of man being tested and purified in the " crucible of God " in order to arrive at his full value for eternity through this test. The Book of Wisdom says of these people: " But the souls of the righteous are in the hand of God . . . God tested them and found them worthy of himself; like gold in the furnace he tried them " (cf. Wis. 3:1–7). Often it is only the temptations to sin which become a test for man and a possibility of proving himself.

Mention has already been made of the hope in future revelation of the salvation of Christians (1:5). In last analysis this means a "revelation of Jesus Christ" himself. The Christians— often so painfully purified—are to be the adornment of Christ when he reveals himself to the whole world in glory on the last day. Our passage shows how deeply and vividly Peter is convinced of the truth of the most intimate bond between Christians and Christ: they are being purified, they are being educated by the heavenly Father, because of the care of the Father for the honor of his only born. God cares for Christ when Christians experience purifying suffering.

*Without having seen him you love him, though you do not now see him you believe in him and rejoice with unutterable and exalted joy. *As the outcome of your faith you obtain the salvation of your souls.*

Peter paints the picture of the second coming of the Lord in glory with majestic and splendid strokes. His wholly personal and fervent love is directed above all to the earthly man of Nazareth, in whose footsteps one can follow (2:21), who dragged the burden of our sins to Golgotha (2:25), by whose bloody weals we have been healed (2:25). A friend and eyewitness speaks, urged by his love of Christ, and it is this that gives these words their warmth. The complete knowledge of the love-worthiness of that human being shines through. Hearing these words one can see once more that clear morning breaking on the western shore of Lake Gennesaret where a rough and in no way sentimental fisherman confessed thrice: "Lord, you know that I love you" (Jn. 21:15-17).

Twice in verses 6-8 there is mention of the exalted joy of Christians notwithstanding that for the time being they must persevere " a little while " in trials. This does not only mean, as one might expect, a future joy in eternal glory, but a radiant joy already realized on earth as well. This happy rejoicing is enkindled on the one hand by our knowledge concerning salvation which, although hidden, is really present; on the other hand, by a joyful anticipation of meeting Christ, whom we in a manner already see although only with the eyes of faith. This joy present on earth is related to eternal bliss somewhat as is the joy of anticipation of children in the course of the 24th of December to the exultation of Christmas Eve. Just as this joy in anticipation is a true joy so there is for us on earth already a true and genuine joy, indescribable, probably only noticeable by the secret rejoicing in the eyes.

The same word " rejoice " is used by Mary when she entered Elizabeth's house (Lk. 1:47), and it is with this rejoicing gladness that the Christians of the young church came together in Jerusalem to break bread (Acts 2:46). In both instances there were anxieties, misunderstandings and slanders caused by the environment. But it appears that joy shines through purest where it has been purified by distress and trials. We encounter this Christian, radiant joy again and again since the first century on the faces of the saints of all epochs. It is the heart of Christianity which Peter touches on here: namely, Christian joy itself in distress. The picture of humanity which emerges here is already the realization of what Jesus had announced in the beatitudes of the Sermon on the Mount (Mt. 5:3-12).

It seems that the earlier announcement of an " inheritance which is imperishable " (1:4) is weakened by the fact that now only " the salvation of your souls " is mentioned. But soul in scripture does not mean, as we sometimes think of it, something purely spiritual, disembodied; rather it signifies the " I," the entire personality. It is this " soul " which Peter, for example, wants " to lay down " for Christ (Jn. 13:37). The fulfillment of the entire personality is at stake, its true life, deliverance and eternal preservation by God. It does not say, " the salvation of your soul " but " the salvation of your souls," for only in union with Christ and in the community of his saints is eternal glory for God's chosen ones possible.

Thanksgiving for the Help of the Holy Spirit (1 : 10–12)

10The prophets who prophesied of the grace that was to be yours searched and inquired about this salvation: 11they inquired what person or time was indicated by the Spirit of Christ within them when predicting the sufferings of Christ and the subsequent glory. 12aIt was revealed to them that they were serving not themselves but you, in the things which have now been announced to you by those who preached the good news to you through the Holy Spirit sent from heaven . . .

Two almost synonymous verbs were chosen to portray the night-long, laborious, yearning meditation, that prayerful inquiry into scripture, of the men of God of the old covenant. They were looking for the messianic time of salvation, that described as Christian salvation. It is significant that no definite " prophet " is mentioned, for the author is not only thinking of named prophets but also of many other holy men who meditate on the law of God by " day and night " (Ps. 1:2). Precisely because a future time of grace has been revealed in the old covenant from the beginning, one always attempted anew to establish the mysterious *when*. The nearer the fullness of time came, the more unquenchable became the desire to see more clearly. And one was convinced that the inquiry into the sacred prophetic writings was a spiritual " preparing the way of the Lord " (Is. 40 : 3) who was awaited. The words from the Book of Henoch written in the second century B.C. could have been the model for our text: ". . . I understood as I saw but not for this generation, but for a remote one which is to come. Concerning the elect I said, and took up my parable concerning them: The holy Great One will come forth from his dwelling . . . and appear in the strength of his might from the heaven of heavens . . . But with the righteous he will make peace and will protect the elect, and mercy shall be upon them and they shall all belong to God and they shall be prospered and they shall all be blessed . . ." (Henoch 1 : 2–8). Many other texts could be quoted which would serve as evidence for the meditative inquiry of scripture and the longing for the Saviour, especially in the last centuries before the appearance of Christ. Only against this living background, still so close to Peter, does it become clear why the reference to the former yearning of the men of God and the present fulfillment forms the climax of the entire grateful song of praise which introduced the letter.

Twice these verses speak of the " spirit " and each time there is an echo of the quite mysterious blowing and breathing of God's life-pneuma. The spirit of God which influenced the prophets of the Old Testament is the spirit of Christ, and the Christian preaching of the apostles occurs by the Holy Spirit of the Lord known from the Old Testament and sent from heaven. For Peter, Christ's activity did not begin when he first appeared in Galilee. Such a view unites the old with the new covenant like a wide bridge-arch. It is Christ who sent the Spirit who spoke through the prophets and it is Christ, also, in whose name the Father poured out his Spirit over the young church at Pentecost.

At that time, on the first morning of Pentecost, it was also Peter who announced to the multitude: The spirit of God prophesied by Joel is the Holy Spirit whom Christ had promised to send (Acts 2:33).

Two truths of the apostolic creed are illuminated by these words: first, the belief that the Holy Spirit had spoken to the world through the prophets from the beginning; secondly, the belief that this Spirit is not only the pneuma of the Father but, at the same time, also of the Son. The life of Christians is drawn into this current of the mysteriously active Spirit of God.

On the way to Emmaus Christ speaks of the suffering and glory of the Messiah foretold in the writings of the prophets (Lk. 24:26). Isaiah clearly portrays the suffering of the servant of God; how he is ill-treated, how he offers his life as a sacrifice for sin (Is. 53:1-11). After this there is immediate mention of his glory: "Therefore, I will divide him a portion with the great, and he shall divide the spoil with the strong; because he poured out his soul to death" (Is. 53:12). Death and glory belong inseparably together in the picture of the servant of God.

What is fascinating in this view is the union of the image of the suffering with that of the glorified Lord. We are to share in his suffering so that we might be participants of his glory (4:13). The character of this letter is the knowledge and recognition of suffering, which sees the cross soberly and without illusion; at the same time, mention of the cross is never separated from the glory of the resurrection, so that the letter maintains an optimistic Christian tone.

12b. . . *things into which angels long to look*.

Overawed at the greatness of the divine plan for salvation, Peter looks upon this happening as a spectacle for heaven. Thus he

concludes the thanksgiving which began the text of the letter in
1:3 with the assurance that even the angels wish to see this
wonderful epoch in the history of God's salvation. In the first
letter to the Corinthians we encounter a similar image. There
the endeavors and battles of the apostolic life are described in a
way suggesting a spectacle in a large Roman amphitheater
with angels sitting in the great circle of the auditorium (1 Cor.
4:9). In Peter's letter, however, angels are not imagined as
spectators in the circles of a theater, but are portrayed as looking
down to earth from heaven. The heavenly sublimity of the angels
and the distance between our and their world appear greater in
this image; at the same time, the impression of their constant
interest even in everyday occurrences becomes more vivid. The
object of the angels' vision is neither a bloody injustice " which
cries to heaven " nor exclusively the liturgical office, but the
entire Christian life hidden or unintelligible to the pagan environment; or, expressed more truly, " the suffering and glory " of
Christ who lives on in the church.

Christian Life—The True Exodus of Israel (1:13—2:10)

From grateful joy at our salvation, moral obligations emerge.
These are expounded in the images of the exodus of Israel from
Egypt, and reappear in the baptismal instructions of the young
church.

Gird Yourselves Hopefully (1:13)

13*Therefore gird up your minds, be sober, set your hope fully* *on the grace that is coming to you at the revelation of Jesus Christ.*

After the jubilation and enthusiasm there is suddenly quite a different note. Precisely because of the salvation that has been imparted to us we ought to be sober. Rejoicing and sobriety belong together in Christianity. The joy of the Holy Spirit is a " sober exuberance," which is essentially different from all enthusiasm of a non-Christian religion and culture. The quiet, supernatural joy of the Holy Spirit makes man internally strong to take in hand a great life's task. For that reason the first exhortation is joined to the previous verse by " therefore ": Because you are now strong in this joy, be prepared. Gird yourselves up. And be sober. This last word emphasizes still further the idea of strengthening and preparation for battle and trial.

The metaphor girding up conjures up in our minds that holy night in which once a community prepared itself for a great journey: " In this manner you shall eat it: your loins girded, your sandals on your feet . . ." (Ex. 12:11). At these words, girding up, that basic note which already sounded quietly in 1:2 and which will dominate the whole section as far as 2:10 is more strongly intoned: the theme of the exodus of the people of Israel from Egypt. But this metaphor girding up is not only meaningful in view of a journey. The ancient garment had also to be tucked up at work as many Roman illustrations of working slaves show. As a working shepherd, Christ also was portrayed from earliest times with tucked up garments.

Of course, it is a spiritual battle, this work and wandering which is at issue here. In a daring image, therefore, Peter speaks of a girding up of the " mind." What is at issue here is the whole of man's volition. his deepest drives. These are to be

mobilized for a life's journey on which the wanderer is motivated
by the hope of the return of the Lord.

Become Holy (1 : 14–16)

14*As obedient children, do not be conformed to the passions of
your former ignorance;* 15*but as he who called you is holy, be
holy yourselves in all your conduct;* 16*since it is written, " You
shall be holy, for I am holy."*

To the image of girding that of conduct is added. The Greek
concept is more expressive. It comprehends more or less what
we mean by " mode of life," and it has the added meaning of
" conversion " or " return." Thus in scripture it also implies
that conversion which is a return to God, from an estrangement.
The journey of the people of Israel from Egypt to the promised
land is a prototype of our return home from the land of sin, of
our moral endeavors.

Since all sin in last analysis is a disobedience, the return
from the land of sin can only be begun by listening to the voice
of the Father calling, that is, by obedience. The " wanderers "
who have set out are addressed as " obedient children." This
obedience begins for Christians on the day of their baptism. They
are to follow the call of God and go his ways even when, from
their manner of thinking, or through human fear, they would
prefer to choose another route.

Every human being wishes to be of value in the world, and
therefore he conforms to the spirit of the times, in his conduct,
in his pleasures, and in his spending for luxuries and distrac-
tions. This former conformity, whereby playing a role before

others stands in the foreground, is to be given up by the recipients of the letter who had been converted from paganism to Christianity—and by us, too, who are still a long way off from living true Christian lives. The letter leaves no doubt that we must keep apart from our surroundings in many things, even in seemingly only external things, ready though we must be to coöperate positively in the social and political spheres of the world in which we live (2:13-17). The theme of being strangers, which was already hinted at in the address (1:1), is clearly discernible here.

Peter conceives the former unbelieving life of the Christians as a time of ignorance. He is convinced that any man who was permitted to recognize God's true being must change his life. In scripture, knowledge of God is often synonymous with worship of God, which finds its expression not only in public worship but above all in the sanctification of one's life.

This has brought us to the main theme: become holy. Christians of the most diverse social standing, these people whom God has called to a great way are to become holy on this journey and by means of this journey, by their "conduct" on the way. The one called must show himself worthy of the one who calls. God is the holy one absolutely, the one who is unapproachable, separate and radiantly pure, whose symbols are light and fire. He is separated from all that is ungodly and impure. The endeavors of late Judaism, above all in priestly circles, with its regulations for separateness and purity only become intelligible on this background: the people must correspond to the totally different, totally pure, totally separate God and become worthy to worship him.

The apostolic letter quotes verbatim the beginning of the laws for holiness in Leviticus. It is to be enforced anew for the faith-

ful of the new covenant. In the third month of the exodus
after the Israelites had reached the Sinai desert, they camped at
the foot of God's mountain. But Moses climbed the mountain
and the Lord spoke to him: "Say to all the congregation of
the people of Israel, You shall be holy; for I the Lord your
God am holy!" (Lev. 19:2). A rabbinic explanation reveals the
deepest meaning of this law: "When you sanctify yourself I
shall reckon it as if you sanctified me, and when you do not
sanctify yourself I shall reckon it as if you do not sanctify me."
This exhortation, then, is identical with that great concern for
which Jesus in the first place asks us to pray: "Hallowed be thy
name" (Mt. 6:9).

Looking back on these verses (1:14-16) the following picture
emerges: To the chosen strangers, whom Peter exhorts to gird
themselves full of hope (1:13) for a march, he announces the
destination of the march: that sanctity which represents one's
own holiness. Since becoming holy means for man a grateful
childlike association with God, having freed oneself from god-
lessness, it represents the highest praise of God. This our most
beautiful task in life is not completed by words but by deeds.
Peter indicates the way: to free oneself of former passions and
of one's own desires and to "follow" on the paths of God: *as
obedient children become holy.*

Be Willing to Obey (1: 17–21)

[17]*And if you invoke as Father him who judges each one imparti-
ally according to his deeds, conduct yourselves with fear throughout the time of your exile.*

Again we are reminded of the child-father relationship, again everything stands under the sign of conduct and pilgrimage, and again the spirit of obedience is evoked; for that is what is basically meant by " conduct yourselves with fear." The Old Testament does not possess a word of its own for " obedience," but presents this basic virtue by various paraphrases, mostly by the expression " fear of God." Thus the fear of God is dealt with like the knowledge of God. The commandment of holiness reminds us of the words of the Lord: " Hallowed by thy name." " Conduct yourselves with fear " may be compared with the third plea in the Lord's Prayer, " Thy will be done."

It is not arbitrary that we relate this text with the Our Father. Not only once, as, for instance, at the moment of baptism, are Christians solemnly to call God " Father," but again and again indeed daily ought they to call God their *Father*. The picture of the heavenly Father which Jesus evoked in the parable at the sea of Gennesaret is less recognizable in this text than is the Old Testament father image. There the father is the commanding authority who teaches the children the laws of the Lord. Already at the beginning of the letter (1 : 2) this great image of an all-wise and all-powerful Father becomes visible, hence it retains its significance also in Christianity. This is the Father whom the church has in mind in nearly all its liturgical prayers.

The wish to fulfill God's will daily by deeds becomes especially intelligible if we remember that God does not take note of externals or of beautiful words, but of the quiet, often hidden, fulfillment of everyday duties. There can be no doubt that, for Peter, only those faithful can stand before God whose faith proves itself in deeds. Everyone will be judged " according to his deeds."

[18]*You know that you were ransomed from the futile ways*

inherited from your fathers, not with perishable things such as silver or gold, ¹⁹*but with the precious blood of Christ like that of a lamb without blemish or spot.*

The special beauty of this passage lies in the words " you know." The letter does not draw out at length that this thought on Christ's blood should result in heartfelt love and gratitude. It only names the facts, it quietly leaves the inferences to us. What are these facts?

To begin with, it is to remain in our minds that we are ransomed from the futile ways inherited from our forefathers. The word " ransom " lets one think not only on the payment of a price, but also on the liberation from misery and shame, at the risk of one's own person, indeed, even of one's blood. Like a poor maid whom a mighty Lord chose as a bride, Israel —a prototype of us—was ransomed from Egypt. Secondly, we are to remember the blood of the lamb. Israel had languished in Egyptian slavery. In the last of the ten plagues the whole of Egypt was to be punished by God in the loss of each first-born. To remain unharmed Israel could not offer God a ransom in money. God wanted to free them " free of charge," not for silver and gold. The paschal lamb took over the sacrifice in place of the first-born of Israel, to appease the Lord. The angel passed by, he passed over the houses where the blood of the paschal lamb dripped from the doorposts. We also have been bought dearly.

For us the sacrificed lamb is Christ. He has become like to the unblemished paschal lamb in Egypt. This lamb is without blemish or spot. The first expression signifies an unobjectionable sacrificial quality in the animal; the second refers to a spiritual, moral characteristic of man. Thus the image of the " lamb

without blemish or spot " stands under a double light: it is
reminiscent of the prototype, the paschal lamb, as also of the
original, the death on the cross. At the same time the total
physical and spiritual beauty of the son of man is illuminated.
That which follows the word " you know " becomes more and
more the deepest reason for the fear of God in conduct; for the
" fearful " demonstration of God's love becomes ever more
clearly visible.

[20]*He was destined before the foundation of the world but was
made manifest at the end of the times for your sake.* [21]*Through
him you have confidence in God, who raised him from the dead
and gave him glory, so that your faith and hope are in God*

Christ moves still more centrally into the focus of the meditation.
After the bloody passion had been mentioned, Peter is urged
to speak also of the resurrection. Christ in his passion and
through his vicarious expiatory suffering as paschal lamb has
become the " duke " in his resurrection, that is the one who
precedes the liberated victoriously. The hope, the firm security
of all, is attached to him. Behind the triumphant final sentence
stands the knowledge of the worth of representative suffering
first recognized by Isaiah. Only he who has first taken on himself
sin which separates us from God, and has removed it as an
impediment, can truly lead us to hope, victory, and eternal life
in union with God. Thus Christ was " predestined " to be the
lamb of God from eternity. In the fullness of time he was
revealed, when the Baptist of the Jordan pointed towards Jesus
with the words: " Behold, the Lamb of God " (Jn. 1 : 29.36).

For your sake God was revealed. The communities in those
days understood this " for your sake " rightly, and to this day

the apostolic church professes: " Who for us men and for our salvation came down from heaven . . . and was crucified also for us . . . ." Christ became the possibility of man to attain to a bond with God. " Through him " salvation was achieved, whereby the " through " designates the way from and to the Father, as also the active coöperation of Christ. The entire story of salvation is centered on Christ. The singular position of the Father who " raised him " and " gave him glory," which is strongly emphasized in this letter, does not minimize the central and kingly position of Christ as the " slain lamb," whom the multitude honors (Rev. 5:12).

Love One Another (1:22–25)

²²*Having purified your souls by your obedience to the truth for a sincere love of the brethren, love one another earnestly from the heart.*

The idea of obedience, so decisive for Peter, is taken up once more and receives here a more precise definition as " obedience to the truth." The meaning of this phrase is simply: " in true obedience." This means an actual, genuine and honest obedience and attention to God and his will: a life which has taken God's commandments seriously. The promise at baptism to obey was only the external expression of this inner, fundamental attitude, which proves itself in deeds.

Previously, obedience in everyday life was recommended as the simplest and best way to sanctity (1:14-16). Here the endeavors at personal holiness are already presupposed. Peter writes: " Having purified your souls " (so that you now are holy). He remains within the framework of his great simile, whereby the life of Christians is seen to be the true exodus of Israel from Egypt. Thereby the word " purify " reminds one of the cult of purification of God's people before their great hour of destiny at Sinai. It is reported of them that at the foot of God's mountain they washed themselves, purified themselves, and kept themselves ready for their encounter with Yahweh. A life modeled on Christ, which sees the will of God precisely in acceptance of difficulties, is for the Christian that purification and sanctification which the Israel of the Old Testament tried to achieve at Sinai by washings and abstentions.

But this sanctification occurs by " a sincere love of the brethren." For that is, as it were, the " first " will of God. He who has become obedient and is well on the way to sanctification recognizes that all deeds converge in love. The emptier the Christian becomes of himself in abstinence and renunciation, the freer he will become for brotherly love. Therefore, it is a command here: Christians are to love one another " earnestly," love one another with an intense, constant love, which is founded in the love of God. Our love ought to be as indefatigable and sincere as our prayers.

[23]*You have been born anew, not of perishable seed but of imperishable, through the living and abiding word of God;* [24]*for " All flesh is like grass and all its glory like the flower of grass. The grass withers and the flower falls,* [25]*but the word of the Lord abides for ever." That word is the good news which was preached to you.*

The presupposition for membership of the new family as brother or sister is a renewed spiritual birth, a new beginning to life.

Once already our letter has considered the very decisive moment of a new beginning (1:3). The Israelites of the Old Testament had also undergone such a moment in which new life was given to them by the word of the Lord, at Sinai. The old commentators understood that moment not only in the sense of grace, that the Israelites remained alive in that encounter with God, were not destroyed by the power and the might of God, but above all in the sense that they were presented with new life through their covenant with God and his law. The situation of Christians is comparable to this. God has addressed them with power, they also were smitten by his word when with Jesus they first came into contact with the " living word of God " (Heb. 4:12). The encounter between man and Christ is a matter of life and death, as it was for Israel at Sinai. He who believes and is subject to the law of Christ has been given life for the second time.

Many texts of early Christian times show that it was not only baptism which was conceived as a rebirth, but also the first conscious hearing of the gospel, the good news of the death and resurrection of Jesus of Nazareth. Readers may remember the hour when they for the first time listened to a sermon which touched their hearts; something like this occurs every time we listen to the word of salvation and accept it.

The train of thought in this passage is as follows : When you heard of Jesus Christ you began to be new human beings. You endeavoured to live a true Christian life and to free yoursleves from your vices. Now, you must crown this development with a growth in Christian love. The individual experience of the first affirmation and the work of one's own self, different for every person, ought to have for its purpose the community in love, which is, in last analysis, the church.

The exhortation flows over into a joyful announcement of the heights and depths of a life with Christ by referring to good news. The word of God originates from the book of consolation of the prophet Isaiah (Is. 40 : 6–8). Indeed, all flesh is miserable, weak grass, but God is constant and stable. And this is followed by the command of God: Get you up to the mountain and let this flesh rejoice, announce to this flesh, announce to this abject grass the good tidings: " Behold your God." Behold the Lord comes with might. But not only with might, he also comes as a shepherd who carries even the weak lambs in his arms (cf. Is. 40 : 9–11). And our final verse speaks of this eternal word of God, of this promise of God to come to man as king and shepherd: That has been accomplished in you. That is the word announced to you, the life-giving good news.

Long for the Word of God Like Thirsty Infants (2 : 1–3)

¹*So put away all malice and all guile and insincerity and envy and all slander.* ²*Like newborn babes long for the pure spiritual milk that by it you may grow up to salvation;* ³*for you have tasted the kindness of the Lord.*

Again Peter sees the people of Israel at the mountain of Sinai as a " prototype " of the Christian community. They are the people that God got to know, to whom God began to speak. By this they became children before God. They have begun to thirst, not only like Israel in the wilderness for the water from the rock, but they even need milk. Peter frankly seeks an image which speaks even more distinctly of the new childhood of Christians. They are to be like " newborn babes," who have begun to cry for their mother's breast. He calls to them: Yes, drink, long avidly for this genuine, the only strengthening and sustaining, nourishment.

But they are not only small children because they have been born anew through the word of God, but also because they put away all malice and guile and now like small children they are humble and innocent disciples of Christ for whom alone the kingdom of God stands open. Here the two concepts of the small child held by the young church converge. From being men of the world the Christians, these citizens and slaves, wives and husbands, presbyters and clerics are to become humble and pure children by renouncing all malice. And on the other hand, from this childhood, newly won by faith in Christ, they are to grow up to the fullness of their Christian calling. The same people who in our text are compared to " newborn babes " are addressed a few verses further on as " a holy nation," a " kingly priesthood " (2:9). The emphasis lies not on the still brief term of existence but on the longing for the truth of God.

For the babe, the mother's milk is the daily bread in which the mother gives herself. God, whose love for us is compared with the love of a mother for her small child, gives himself to humanity in his own Son, the eternal Logos. The original text, therefore, calls this milk the Logos-milk. It is Jesus Christ himself whom the recipients have accepted in their hearts with the word of the good news in order to strengthen themselves in him and on him . . . But even in those days there were false teachers who offered watered-down milk. The " pure " milk, however, is the apostolic preaching of Christ which has for its center the historical report of his suffering.

Whenever a man takes seriously what the gospel preaches, his life will change unwittingly. He will as it were change his clothing. To be sure, what is to be put off are not often notorious vices like murder, theft, or fornication; but more often such things as secret dishonesty and lovelessness. Specifically mentioned, for instance, is insincerity, all those small attempts we make to be regarded as better than we are; and also slander, the many uncharitable words we say about our neighbors. The clothing is here a symbol of the moral traits of man. A marvelous optimism is expressed in this symbolism. Sin is regarded as something which man can truly " put away " like a dress, so that his inner being, which in no way is rotten to the core but rather is good, can appear.

Then another final justification is given for this exhortation: Just as for the babe the appetite for his mother's milk comes at the first tasting, Christians' longing should grow more and more since they have tasted once what it is to be a Christian. They have now broken through the thickets of Jewish and heathen misunderstandings and have known what the Lord Jesus Christ is in reality.

Let Yourselves be Built (2 : 4–6)

[4]*Come to him, to that living stone, rejected by men but in God's sight chosen and precious;* [5]*and like living stones be yourselves built into a spiritual house, to be a holy priesthood, to offer spiritual sacrifices acceptable to God through Jesus Christ.*

" To him " refers to " Lord " in the previous verse, whom the wanderers had tasted as a libation. Not only the drink but also the rock out of which the water streams is Christ. This rock has now become a fashioned building stone, indeed, a foundation stone, that cornerstone in the building's foundation on which the alignment of the walls, the cohesion, and stability of the building depend. Those who come out of the " darkness of Egypt " are to travel to that living stone. Two extreme contrasts are bound up in the image of the living stone: the hardness of a rock and pulsating life—the truth of God eternally faithful to itself and the love of God. This great, fundamental building stone of God was cast out of the building site as worthless and irksome by the builders. But precisely this stone, worthless from an earthly viewpoint, has become in God's eyes the valuable stone.

The other stones are to become like the living foundation stone. Perhaps they will also be rejected by men. But it is precisely such tested, living stones the Father would like to build on to his fundamental, first cornerstone. For this they are to be prepared: to let themselves be squared by God and be fitted into the frame of the other living stones. In biblical thought the concept " build " in no way signifies a dead mechanical process. Thus, for instance, God " built " Eve out of Adam's rib (Gen. 2:22), to David he promised " to build a house " for his offspring (2 Sam. 7:11). Hence the transposition from the physical to the spiritual building of a community of men would naturally suggest itself. And from there it is only a small step to these words of Jesus addressed to Peter which we are to overhear in this passage: " You are Peter, and on this rock I will build my church " (Mt. 16:18).

The " spiritual house " built from " living stones " is a " holy priesthood." Those words are addressed to different classes, professions, ages and sexes. To be a member of the church means to become a priest. How can Peter call a community a community of priests? The answer lies in the same verse: all are to offer sacrifices. If we question further, namely, what these sacrifices are, we need not look far. Already this letting-oneself-be-built as stones, letting-oneself-be-tested, as Christ was, means a tremendous sacrifice, pleasing to the Father. For God's temple can only incorporate building stones which, through humility, obedience, and consideration for the construction of this eternal dwelling of the community of saints, are suitable. In the priesthood of Christian life, which begins with baptism, the entire man should, as it were, give himself as a building stone to the master builder.

⁶*For it stands in scripture: " Behold I am laying in Sion a stone, a cornerstone chosen and precious, and he who believes in him will not be put to shame."*

The author does not use the Old Testament (Is. 28:16) at first hand, but probably some ancient Christian collection of texts from prophets that seemed especially important to the catechists of the apostolic times. The quotation diverges from the text of the Greek Old Testament also in the text form. On the other hand, this divergence tallies with Romans 9:33. The authors of Romans and 1 Peter seem to have had the same copy before them.

The insecurity of lies and the fickleness of egotism and of infirm belief will stop when a living faith is firmly anchored on that rock. Having become anchored in a firm belief, such people begin to participate in the stability of God. And such divine, permanent stability remains faithful. When after death all greatness solely founded on earthly success and earthly power is reduced to nothingness, then the great hour will come for the believer who has already begun to participate in the stability of the house of God. He will not be " ashamed " to have believed in the crucified, in the stone rejected by the mortal architects.

Summing up: God's Holy People (2:7–10)

⁷*To you therefore who believe, he is precious, but for those who do not believe, " The very stone which the builders rejected has become the head of the corner " *⁸ᵃ*and "A stone that will make men stumble, a rock that will make them fall"; for they stumble because they disobey the word,*

The six exhortative requests (1:13—2:6) have now been concluded. Now begin the great final statements of the first main section, which almost brim over into a hymn. To begin with, there is another short reference to the fact that those who believe participate in the honor of the cornerstone, rejected by men and all the more valuable to God. Then, however, Peter turns his attention to the fatalistic fact that this cornerstone, the deepest and foremost stone in God's building, can become " *a stone that will make men stumble,*" indeed, can become a stone against which the waves of ungodly storms break. What seems to be at stake here is that tragic experience that for some the incarnation of God can be the cause of their damnation because they will not accept it in faith. What is in mind is that mystery of which the old Simeon had a prophetic vision as he held the child in his arms in the temple and said: " Behold this child is set for the fall and rising of many in Israel, and for a sign that is spoken against " (Lk. 2:34).

⁸ᵇ. . . *as they were destined to do.*

In the letter of Barnabas this stone which makes men stumble was Christ in the flesh (being slapped in the face by the Jews and mocked by the cohorts). The executioners of Jesus were, in accordance with God's counsel, destined to do this: destined to be angered with Jesus, to deliver him up, and out of envy and hate to give him over to be crucified.

With absolute sovereignty God seems to place men and destinies as black and white figures on the chessboard of history. Yet in spite of being placed thus the responsibility of the individual remains unimpaired. Indeed, precisely this freedom of man to be able to act against God's will is made use of by God in his plans. We shall never on this earth be able to understand the mystery of human free will which seems to be only truly free when it participates in God's absolute free will.

⁹But you are a chosen race, a royal priesthood, a holy nation, God's own people, that you may declare the wonderful deeds of him who called you out of darkness into his marvelous light.

Without wishing to replace the Israel of the old covenant by something different, the true fulfillment of all the ancient hopes of Israel is proclaimed. The Christian communities are addressed by the great honorary titles of the people of God. They are a " chosen race." They are the same people who were at the beginning addressed as chosen strangers (1:1). Seen with the eyes of faith, they form the holy remainder of the end of the messianic period, that flock traveling through the desert under the leadership of a great shepherd, the object of the Father's love and care. The first honorary title, a " chosen race," intimates that text of Isaiah which dominates the entire verse: " For I give water in the wilderness, rivers in the desert, to give drink to my chosen people, the people whom I formed for myself that they might declare my praise " (Is. 43:20f.).

Above (2:5) there was mention of a " holy " priesthood; here royal priests, or kings who are also priests, are addressed. Such royalty, such belonging to the race of kings also includes the power to rule. Such a power to rule is referred by Peter to the life of Christians: they are to rule over themselves. Hence even in these glorious titles there is intimated something of the basic anxiety that permeates the entire letter, to exhort those in his care. But this barely audible exhortation is wholly embedded in the consoling declaration of the true greatness of every baptized Christian.

Our text concerning the royal priesthood has quite rightly at all times been regarded as the most important basis for the Catholic teaching on universal priesthood. It is significant that in the whole of the New Testament only Jesus Christ himself is called a priest. The superiors of communities are called merely guardians, or elders. It is all the more astonishing that all Christians, without exception, are declared to be a royal priesthood. The young church possessed a lively conviction that all chosen people, men or women, educated or uneducated, have their priestly function in the liturgy celebrated in common, that they " celebrate " together. Exodus states of all Israelites: There at Sinai the whole of Israel became a race of priests, because it was enabled to take on the service of mediator for the whole of humanity. All baptized people received the same power for the humanity in the midst of which we live. At the same time, these words concerning the priestly duty of all the members of the church in regard to the world contain the most beautiful justification for the missionary activities of every Christian.

All preceding honorary titles are somehow once more summed up in the thought that Christians are God's property which he has altogether personally reserved for himself, a people which is his very own, a community which has the task as a pure, holy, priestly, royal people to glorify God precisely through this holiness. They are there to prove by their lives that God's powerful intervention in the innermost recesses of the human ego can make saints out of sinners—even out of former enemies of God.

The wonderful deed of God for his people consists of having led human beings out of darkness into light. For the last time the theme of Israel's exodus from Egypt is intoned in these words about the call out of darkness. In this final exultation there is even talk about a call out of darkness into his " marvelous light." Right at the end of the letter the same occurrence is described as a call " to his eternal glory " (5:10). Both light and glory are now a reality, are the world in which we live considered as an earthly fact. We are called to become radiantly happy, royal, self-controlled priests for humanity.

[10]*Once you were no people but now you are God's people; once you had not received mercy but now you have received mercy.*

The present time is distinct from the past in that God has now given his mercy. But it is important for Peter to emphasize that once they were no people, but they have now been called to be the people of God, to form this people of God itself. The prophet Hosea had to call his two children at first " Not pitied " and " Not my people " (Hos. 1:6-9). But then the same prophet tells movingly how God's love—like that of a bridegroom—turns once more to the cast-off bride: " And I will have pity on Not pitied, and I will say to Not my people, ' You are my people '; and he shall say, ' Thou art my God.' " (Hos. 2:24). The church is the " chosen people ": the people who are to increase, who shall remain firm in battle, who shall be afflicted by sicknesses and inner unrests, but who will never stop being pitied.

THE RESPONSIBILITIES OF THOSE CALLED
(2:11—4:11)

The introductory section (1 : 3—2 : 10) finished with a joyful, uplifting and enthusiastic portrayal of the state in which Christians find themselves. With the address " beloved " something new begins. Not till 4 : 12 will the recipients be once more addressed with the same word "beloved." What lies in between constitutes the main part of the letter. In it we are exhorted and encouraged by a manifold reference to the example of Christ.

General and Basic Counsels (2:11–12)

Before he deals with particular exhortations, Peter points to the basic meaning of sacrifice, abstention, and good works. They are advantageous to one's own soul and are, at the same time, the most effective means of opening the eyes of a sceptically observing heathen world to God's truth.

Personal Abstentions (2 : 11)

11Beloved, I beseech you as aliens and exiles to abstain from the passions of the flesh that wage war against your soul.

The letter address " beloved " without any addition was unknown in the antique world before the first Christian letters were written. It arises from the knowledge that all Christians have been born anew and so have become beloved brothers (1 : 22f). Not their good characteristics but the greatness of him who loved them made them worthy of love. And for that reason he to whom the care of the Lord's flock was entrusted, having been questioned concerning his love (Jn. 21 : 15–17), loves them with all his heart. This first personal mode of address in the letter has vividly and almost necessarily grown out of the enthusiasm of 29f. Here the spirit, which inspires the whole of this pastoral letter (2 : 25), this first Roman " encyclical " in the history of the church, becomes tangible. Out of this spirit of loving care spring the following urging, exhorting, encouraging words.

We take away the real significance of the text if for " passions of the flesh " we immediately understand moral vices. The young church's immediate understanding of the desire of the flesh was something different. In the so-called " Teaching of the Twelve Apostles," after the New Testament the oldest writing of Christendom, there is the warning in verbal harmony with our letter: " abstain from passions of the flesh and of the body." And after that there follows, as an explanation of what this abstention means, an account of the instructions of the Sermon on the Mount: To him who strikes you on the right cheek turn also your left cheek; if any one forces you to go a thousand steps, go with him two thousand steps; and if any one wants your coat, let him have your cloak as well. The passion of the flesh then consists chiefly of self-love, the greatest enemy of the soul. This first basic exhortation paves the way for the particular exhortation to humble submission and to the renunciation of self-assured pride, without which all striving for perfection is but empty froth.

An Exemplary Way of Life (2:12)

¹²*Maintain good conduct among the gentiles, so that in case they speak against you as wrongdoers, they may see your good deeds and glorify God on the day of visitation.*

They are to prove themselves worthy of their station as royal priests not only interiorly, but also visibly (2:12). They are to " conduct " themselves so well that it attracts the attention of others. Without a doubt there is the danger of hypocrisy when such importance is attached to externals. Numerous condemnations of hypocritical Pharisees, recorded in the gospels, are a warning to Christians of this dangerous temptation. We are to preach with works which must be a radiation of the soul's inner nobility. And experience teaches that preaching by deeds is more important and more successful than preaching by words, which without deeds is almost worthless. The final aim of preaching through good works lies not in winning heathens for Christianity, but in increasing the glory and praise of God " on the day of visitation." This day on which God is especially concerned with men and visits them in mercy or in anger is the last judgment day, this terrible and, at the same time, splendid final act in the drama of God's story of man's salvation. Whether these slanderers will change their ways before that time is not mentioned explicitly. It is desirable that this change should begin while they are still able to observe the Christians in this earthly life. But, perhaps, the eyes of those who now live as if there were no " day of visitation " for them will be opened in astonishment for the first time on that day. The text leaves this question open. Not an earthly but an eternal success is the important thing in our endeavors.

The Christian Weekday (2:13—3:12)

After the general instruction to wage war against self-love and
to conduct one's life so that it is exemplary also externally, the
concrete exhortations begin: to be subject to the institution of
the state (2:13–17); servants, to be submissive to their masters
(2:18–25); wives, to be submissive to their husbands, and
husbands to be considerate to their wives (3:7). An exhortation
for all to be humble in dealing with one another, and to forgive
one another (3:8–12) concludes this section, which gives an insight second to none into the everyday life of the young church.
Together with the portrayal of the Lord's example, it belongs
to the most beautiful parts of our letter.

Be Subject to the State (2:13–17)

[13]*Be subject for the Lord's sake to every human institution,
whether it be to the emperor as supreme* [14]*or to the governors as
sent by him to punish those who do wrong and to praise those
who do right.* [15]*For it is God's will that by doing right you
should put to silence the ignorance of foolish men.*

For the first time there is talk of the duty of Christians " to be
subject " and to regard themselves as subject. The exhortation to
subject oneself freely, of one's own accord, to a public authority
or to some " lord " of this world is characteristic of this letter,
and it is also a reflection of the teaching of the early Christians.

The question of the relation of the Christian to the state may never be separated from this general Christian ideal of free submission. The Christian virtues of obedience and humility always stand in the foreground. What is valid for submission in political life is equally valid in the family (3 : 1–7) and at the place of work (2 : 18–25).

A double reason for such freely willed subjection was already mentioned: the eternal salvation of the soul and the glory of God (2 : 11f.). A new addition is that it should happen " for the Lord's sake." That means for the sake of the example of a Lord who subjected himself not only to the will of the Father, but who also, by humbling himself, accommodated himself to the questions of Annas and Caiaphas, the whims of Herod and Pilate, the urgings and pleadings of the people, and the thousand questions and idiosyncrasies of the disciples who accompanied him for years. Perhaps these four short words, " for the Lord's sake," also wish to say " for the love of the Lord ": for the love of that Lord whose passion Christians know (2 : 21b–24a), through whose bloody wounds they were healed (2 : 24b), whose nature they recognized with the eyes of faith and whom they began to love gladly as a friend (1 : 8).

The relation of Christians to the Roman state is portrayed in a twofold manner. Already in the beginning of the letter, in the address (1 : 1), a twofold aspect came to light. Christians are, on the one hand, to regard themselves as " sown " in this world so as to bear spiritual fruit in it and in coöperation with it and, on the other hand, they are to think of themselves as " strangers " who indeed live in this world, but have not their home here and who, therefore, can face all state organizations and institutions with an inner freedom. This passage is concerned with the positive relationship of the Christian to the state's authority, that is, with ready coöperation in all just public institutions which are for the welfare of the citizen. Peter is here thinking of a government apparatus which is capable of performing its function. In the provincial cities of the Roman empire, in the early years of the Caesars, the citizen still received the impression of a well-ordered government and of firm discipline. Added to this was the Old Testament tradition that even a pagan state was God's instrument.

Unhesitatingly Peter gives to the king, Caesar, or emperor and his agents the right to punish criminals. In the Letter to the Romans it is stated even more clearly that the ruling authority bears " the sword of judgment " for that purpose (Rom. 13:4). Besides the right to punish, the right of the state to praise and give distinctions is also acknowledged. One must imagine the public honoring of citizens who have been of special service to the community to involve, to a lesser degree, the conferring of decorations as is customary today—such as being entered into the honorary list of a city, or having a statue erected in the market-place. Peter writes of these rights of a pagan state because he wishes that Christians would also do their part in public and even political life. It is plainly God's will (2:15) to prove oneself by good works and industry in public also. A great optimism is suggested here, one which reckons with right-thinking and right-judging men being present everywhere. Of course, the religious practices of Christians will never receive praise anywhere, but it is to be hoped that, at least, no fault will be found with their willingness to work, readiness to help and their commitment to duty. Again there is no mention here of Christian missionary attempts at the place of work or in the neighbourhood by means of high-sounding words (cf. 2:12; 3:1). Deeds are much more effective and persuasive.

[16]*Live as free men, yet without using your freedom as a pretext for evil; but live as servants of God.*

The exhortation to be subject to, and to coöperate with the state is followed, as a complement, by the spirited words of the freedom of Christians in regard to this state. These citizens and businessmen, these officials and soldiers, these tradesmen and housewives, indeed, even the male and female slaves should, in last analysis, always feel as " free men " in regard to the laws and powers of the state. Their freedom is founded on the fact that they belong to a greater master, for whom they were bought like slaves for the price of the blood of Jesus Christ (1:18f.). To him alone are they subject without reservations. His authority has much greater weight than that of the seemingly almighty Roman state. As soon as the commands of any of those public courts of justice contradict the laws of God written in men's hearts they lose their binding force for all who know themselves to be the slaves of God. Perhaps their threatening, fear-inspiring character will not immediately vanish from this. But to the extent that the holy fear of God (2:17), their spiritual slavery, grows in them, their fear of earthly rulers will tend to decrease. The more one becomes the slave of God, the less one will ever feel oneself under earthly compulsions. To serve God will mean spiritual mastery.

[17]*Honor all men. Love the brotherhood. Fear God. Honor the emperor.*

This section concerning the behavior of Christians in public life is concluded by a general principle: In any case, have respect for all men no matter whom. The emphatic final sentence " Honor the emperor," towards which the rest moves, shows that Peter has not yet lost sight of the theme of the submission of Christians to their political rulers. They should give due honor to state officials by subjecting themselves to authority after the example of Christ.

The respect one ought to have for the eternal Father is somewhat different. They should remember that as children and servants he can punish not only temporally, like human beings can, but he can cast them into eternal ruin. Therefore, Jesus says of him: " Fear him " (Mk. 12:5). The highest grade of respect, that is, the fear of God, will find its expression in absolute obedience.

Without stating it explicitly, this kind of enumeration of the different forms of respect makes the boundaries visible which Christian respect may not transcend in its dealings with the mighty of this earth, if it is not to become fawning and flattery. The spirit of respect, therefore, appears as a basic virtue of the rational human being in his relation to God and his entire creation. And the love for the brethren turns out to be a form of such respect which likes to " count others better than oneself " (Philem. 2:3).

The Submission of Household Servants (2:18-25)

THE EXHORTATION (2:18)

[18]*Servants, be submissive to your masters with all respect, not only to the kind and gentle but also to the overbearing.*

After the exhortation to all Christians to be subject to the power of the state the instructions for certain individual groups now

begin. In the first instance the lowest class is addressed. Man-
servants and maids represent for Peter in the purest form the
type of the Christian image of man; for the Christian is the
" servant of God " (2:16) and is most like to Christ in humiliation and suffering (2:21). For that reason only this first exhortation for servants is furnished with the incomparable portrait of
the suffering Lord (2:21b–24) which sounds like an extract from
the gospel account of the passion. The preferential treatment of
these servants and maids seemingly without right or honor is
founded on the main theme of the whole letter, the core of which
begins here: consoling and exhorting, he wants to convince the
reader that suffering, for Christians, is synonymous with being-
in-grace (2:19a, 20b; cf. 5:12).

Servants are to be submissive with all respect to their masters.
Only superficially does this mean that household servants should
comply swiftly with every wink of the master, because they live
in constant fear of punishment. Indeed, in 2:20 there is mention
of the fact that these same Christians fearlessly bear undeserved
beatings; in 3:6 women are explicitly exhorted to be fearless;
and in 3:14 it is again emphasized that the Christian should have
no fear of men. It is not fear of man which is in view here but
fear of God. They are to realize that they are servants not of
earthly masters but of God. To him they must look with holy
respect when they obey the word of earthly masters.

The First Reason: Suffering is Grace (2:19–21a)

[19]*For one is approved if, mindful of God, he endures pain while
suffering unjustly.* [20]*For what credit is it, if when you do wrong
and are beaten for it you take it patiently? But if when you do*

right and suffer for it you take it patiently, you have God's approval.

After the harsh command (2:18) a milder, explanatory tone is now adopted; such an obedience has God's approval, such a person finds grace in God's eyes. What does Peter imagine the situation of the addressees to be? The masters of such servants were at times ill-humored or malevolent, indeed, even vicious or malicious. He is thinking of situations in which a Christian, precisely because he is a Christian, is constantly subjected to small, secretive, spiteful actions. Daily he is exposed to these psychologically unjust vexations which hurt more than beatings. He has worked and has helped and in thanks he is mocked and ridiculed, perhaps because someone has seen him pray once. Soon he is known among the other servants as someone on whom any one may play a practical joke, since neither the housemaster nor his steward will stand up for him. Such is perhaps the situation of those of whom it is said that they begin to radiate a spiritual beauty, and God's eyes rest favorably and with special approval upon them. The entire absurdity of Christian teaching and of the Christian life seems to become tangible.

²¹ª*For to this you have been called . . .*

Peter goes so far as to say that this is the actual aim of conversion to Christianity, the recipients are called to this. There is no doubt concerning the meaning of the passage: accepted spiritual and physical suffering is that condition which is the final aim of God's calling and election on earth. This becomes quite intelligible from other passages in the letter. There the ideal of a holy, royal priesthood, which offers sacrifice for the world, is outlined

(2:5.9). And Peter wishes that his Christians should have this honor. While earlier (2:5) it was stated in the form of a parable that the priestly sacrifice consists of delivering up one's own ego to the great divine master builder as a living building stone, here this royal priestly service receives a more concrete expression: It consists of silently tolerating undeserved vexations and patiently bearing beatings in one's own body. From the " to this " of the text there radiates the dignity of the sacrificial offering of the royal priest. And if we look ahead we already get a glimpse through this " to this " of the picture of that man who bears " in his body " the sins of others to the cross (2:25).

The next phrase (2:21b) shows that we are here dealing with a universally valid statement concerning the highest ideal and deepest meaning of being Christian. It is not the intention here to say that all Christians without exception are called to a life of continuous suffering. In 4:12 it will be said tentatively that we should not regard it strange if we are sometimes tested. But, nonetheless, the letter demonstrates that the glad, even joyful (1:6), willing " sharing in Christ's suffering " (4:13) is the greatest ideal to which a Christian could be called by God. For that means sharing in the royalty and priesthood of Christ.

THE SECOND REASON: CHRIST'S EXAMPLE (2:21b–24)

[21b] . . . because Christ also suffered for you, leaving you an example, that you should follow in his steps.

The last and most precious trump-card which Peter can play in his efforts to project the right concept of the essence of Christianity is the portrayal of the Lord himself as inspired by a loving heart. Through his representative suffering, Christ has given us a living example of what is at stake.

The Greek word for *example* here actually signifies the copy which helps schoolchildren to learn to draw the difficult lines of the individual letters. Also, in difficult, say marshy ground it can be very helpful to possess detailed markings of the course of a narrow path. Perhaps someone has already gone ahead, in whose footsteps we can tread confidently. When it is a question of a climb up a steep mountain wall, the advancing guide will turn around again and again to point out the way. He will show where he himself put the right leg, where he could find a hold for his left hand. He will not choose a route which is too difficult for his followers. He has only one wish: to reach the summit with all together. Therefore they are to follow him exactly and can confidently imitate his example.

Everything that now will be said (2:22–24) concerning the passion of Jesus is to be understood as an example which we are to imitate. If, however, it is all an example, then also is his representative suffering " for you," that is, for us. We also are to advance courageously by silently bearing difficulties for the sake of others who tend to lose heart, and to leave behind footsteps which show the only possible way.

²²*He committed no sin, no guile was found on his lips.*

In the verses beginning here the viewpoint changes always back and forth: from the suffering servants to Christ and from suffering Christ back to the Christians. The picture of the suffering Lord is not only given as an encouraging example but is illuminated in its divine greatness as free from all sin: You servants are indeed scolded for alleged mistakes which you have not made (2:19), but Christ was much more free from any guilt than you. You indeed are beaten (2:20), as if you had been impudent, but from his lips there never came a rebellious, untrue, or spiteful word. You are still battling with your faults (2:11f.), he could say to the entire people and to his disciples, who were with him day and night, " Which of you convicts me of sin?" (Jn. 8:46). And in spite of this complete guiltlessness his Father sent him on the path of suffering so unintelligible to you, on the path of that servant of God whom Isaiah had so movingly described in prophecy.

23a*When he was reviled, he did not revile in return; when he suffered, he did not threaten; . . .*

Before us is a picture of the suffering Christ such as no writer of the New Testament has drawn; a man who is reviled, who is scolded like a menial who did not mind his own business, who is overwhelmed with criticism and invective—and who remains silent. The intense care of Peter for those he wishes to exhort becomes visible, and the total love of the friend of Jesus, who infers the temptation of the Lord in those hours of suffering from his own hot temperament which would like to retaliate immediately, emerges. Indeed, he goes even further and depicts how easy it would have been for the Master to threaten his enemies with the judgment of God. For us also it seems entirely natural to be tempted to call upon the avenging God because of a personal insult. But Peter asks us: Where is your imitation of Christ?

23b*. . . but he trusted to him who judges justly.*

Peter does not refer here to the judgment of Christ before Pilate.

Rather, he wishes to say: Christ trusted himself, that is, his
" case," his entire concern regarding the retribution of the
injustice done to him, to his heavenly Father and gave us, to
whom it is due by far more, an example to leave vengeance to
God (Rom. 12:19). The following verse shows that even more
is at issue. Christ left not only his case to the eternal judge but
also offered himself to the divine anger as a sacrifice for our
sins. He gave a still greater example when he humbly accepted
a judgment to be pronounced against him, which in fact others
deserved. Thus he becomes for us the " word " of God, which is
a signpost for us. We also should, without asking whether we
deserve it or not, be ready to bear suffering, and be aware that
the time has come " for judgment to begin with the household
of God " (4:17), that judgment in which " the righteous man
is scarcely saved " (4:18). The history of mankind, with all its
suffering, which often the innocent must bear, becomes more
intelligible when we see it as a great, terribly serious judgment
on the sin and disobedience of the creature against the creator.

²⁴ᵃ*He himself bore our sins in his body on the tree* . . .

Christ has not only carried the burden of our sins to Golgotha
as the bearer of a sacrifice might carry his sacrificial animal to
the altar, but he has made himself into this sacrificial animal
in his becoming man, by means of his human body as God
incarnate: into a lamb ready for slaughter, who has taken on
himself " the sins of the world " (Jn. 1:29). He has made this
burden of sins so much his own that he became plainly a
" curse " (Gal. 3:13). Peter still sees him, how he dragged
himself to Golgotha, where already visible afar the tree, the
perpendicularly standing wooden stake, jutted out. He remem-

bered how he carried the short crossbeam thither, was nailed to it by the hands, to be then, hanging on the crossbeam, pulled up like a sail on the perpendicular mast. The crimes of others, and those of the addressed servants, he took up with him on this wooden trunk—which becomes an altar—and thereby into the extreme torment of his last hour. Peter no longer is capable of saying " your sins " as he has just said: Christ has left " you " an example. He speaks of " our sins " because he feels himself to be involved. He wishes to be included in this incarnated, selfless love.

24b. . . *that we might die to sin and live to righteousness.*

The accent lies on the positive aim, for which death to sin is a presupposition: that we might live to righteousness. In this also Christ is our example. He lived to righteousness, in that he was ready to suffer for the sins of others, in order thus to re-establish the disturbed order. His love urged him to renew the right, the just relationship between creator and creature. Also for us to live to righteousness means nothing else but to live to love; for Christian love has little to do with feeling, but is closely related to the will to righteousness. It is typical of the sober and yet radically pursued thinking of Peter that for him a life for the sake of one's fellow creature, a life which does not even shrink from the representative bearing of a cross, is no more than a life of righteousness. What is at issue is the just fulfillment of a great commandment: " You shall love the Lord your God with all your heart, and with all your soul, and with all your strength, and with all your mind; and your neighbor as yourself " (Lk. 10:27).

²⁴ᶜ*By his wounds you have been healed.*

The wound here is the stigma which the rod or whip leaves on
the naked back. In Isaiah, the Hebrew word for wound (or
stripe) is derived from " to cause colored stripes " (53:5). We
may overhear this here too. Peter directs the attention of the
servants to the back of Christ, which is so like their own:
immediately after the beatings one sees swollen, red-raw lines,
perhaps also dark red spots of clotted blood; and later the
stripes become blue and green. By such wounds they were
healed as by a bitter medicine. They were formerly ill, perhaps
like that woman to whom Jesus said: " Your faith has saved
you; go in peace " (Lk. 7:50). And the man in whom she
believed is he who later let himself be scourged—also for them.
Perhaps the addressees here will remember that they also were
healed at their baptism, and will in future be more ready to
bear the unjust whiplashes of a steward out of love for others.

END OF THE EXHORTATION (2:25)

²⁵*For you were straying like sheep, but have now returned to the
shepherd and guardian of your souls.*

The focus is on the expansive, rocky pastures of Palestine on
which sheep graze scattered about. The flock is no longer closely
together. Many sheep have begun to look for patches of grass
on out-of-the-way slopes. The careful shepherd who knows that
such self-willed straying sheep, straying about on their own, are
exposed to the greatest danger of beasts of prey, wants to gather
his flock together once more. To do this it is not necessary to run

after each single sheep and drive it back with the stick. It is sufficient to make an angry attack on any one sheep of the scattered
flock. Immediately the others will also hurry back. Peter sees
Christ as one among these sheep in the midst of the straying
sheep. God the Father, the eternal shepherd, collects his scattered
flock. The sheep, however, who is singled out by the disciplinary
beatings, intended in reality for all the disobedient sheep, is the
innocent " lamb of God." While the strokes of the stick slap
down on his back the whole flock, ashamed in the realization of
its disobedience, rushes back to the right path. They recognize by
the hardness of the discipline which the one animal had to bear
how stupid and wrong their self-willed ways were.

Then Peter adds another sentence in which one can discern
more forcefully the authority of the Apostle. These straying sheep,
these people who once lived without any real spiritual roots, have
returned to their shepherd and guardian. In the first place God
the Father is implied here. He is, indeed, that shepherd who
took on the scattered sheep through the Incarnation of his Son
on whom he heaped all punishment. But the Son is not excluded.
Christians are subject to him as the " chief shepherd " (5 : 4). This
shepherd and " guardian " (*episkopos*) is, however, visibly represented among them by the person whom Christ commanded:
" Feed my lambs " (Jn. 21 : 15–17). Indeed, Peter also knows
other representatives of the chief shepherd: " Guardians," who
no longer receive their mission immediately from God to tend
" the flock of God " in the Holy Spirit (5 : 2; 1 : 12). None of
these three aspects can be excluded. He who can gratefully ascer-
tain that he has found his way to the " bishop " who is visible on
earth, belongs thereby to the flock of Christ (5 : 4) and is safe in
the caring (5 : 7) if sometimes disciplining (4 : 12) protection of the
Father.

The Duties of Wives (3:1–6)

BE SUBMISSIVE (3:1–2)

[1]*Likewise you wives, be submissive to your husbands, so that some, though they do not obey the word, may be won without a word by the behavior of their wives . . .*

It is the main aim of the letter to console, exhort, and encourage Christians tried by suffering. Thus it becomes understandable why wives are addressed in the second place in this catalog of duties. To be sure they are not of the poorer classes like the slaves. What follows shows that Peter also had well-to-do women in mind, women who know how to choose clothes tastefully and to deck themselves with gold ornaments (3:3). In spite of this they are near to slaves: In accordance with the ancient order of society they too are subject absolutely to the commands of the head of the family. From this there stem for them much pain, much worry, and much suffering. And thereby they are also especially close to Christ. Like the slaves, the housewives also came chiefly with their spiritual distress to the priests of the community. Their questions may well have been these: Why am I so unhappy in my marriage? Why do I have to bear all this? How should I behave towards my husband?

To this the Apostle gives the liberating answer: A Christian wife by her example can have a greater influence on her husband than an apostle who preaches the good tidings orally. Christian women are throughout preëminently capable of missionary work. Indeed, even those heathen men who would listen to no sermon are influenced by the life of a woman. They will glean a word from the quiet fulfillment of duty, a word which is basically a part of the eternal Word of the Father which has taken on flesh and which dwells in these Christian women.

² *. . . when they see your reverent and chaste behavior.*

Chaste behavior will convince such hard men. The word " chaste " here means morally without reproach, pure and continent. One would think that this verse suggests the practical experience of the Apostle, who as a husband must have been devoted to his wife with special love and veneration. He knows that nothing more attracts and ennobles a man, even the coarsest, than a wife who values her chastity.

THE ORNAMENT OF WOMEN (3:3-4)

³*Let not yours be the outward adorning with braiding of hair, decoration of gold and wearing of robes, *⁴*but let it be the hidden person of the heart with the imperishable jewel of a gentle and quiet spirit, which in God's sight is very precious.*

Peter does not say that adorning is as such reprehensible. His lucid position differs from other more rigorous exhortations of his time. It is not his wish to forbid women to adorn themselves. What is important to him is to draw the attention of women, who have a sense and taste of true beauty, to the fact that there exists a more refined adornment which becomes them more. That adornment possesses a constant value, independent of fashion, precious even in God's sight. Usually jewels, pearls, and gems are pronounced " precious." All these earthly adornments are only a shadow, a presentiment of the eternal adornment with which a Christian woman will shine forth to "the glory and honor of Jesus Christ on the last day" (1:7). This truly precious and magnificent picture of humanity, one which never fails to attract, which is here brought to women's attention, had already been proclaimed by Christ when he pointed to himself saying: "Learn from me; for I am gentle and lowly in heart, and you will find rest for your souls" (Mt. 11:29). Peter is not afraid that the missionary success of women will be put in jeopardy by their transferring their interest to an inner "beauty culture."

The Example of Great Women (3:5–6)

⁵So once the holy women who hoped in God used to adorn themselves and were submissive to their husbands . . .

Humility, meekness, silent endurance are precious ornaments with which great women always knew how to adorn themselves. Holiness has a beauty all its own, a charm which is incomparable. The ancestral women of Christ, those holy women of the old covenant, radiated such holiness: Rebekah, who humbly offers to draw water also for the camels of the stranger (Gen. 24:18–20); Ruth, who suffers in faithful love to stay with her mother-in-law and modestly gleans ears of corn in the field (Ruth 1:16f.; 2:2–17); or Hannah, who silently turns to the Lord in her distress (1 Sam. 1:10f.). "Holy" does not mean here only "chosen" or "belonging to God," but truly an "exemplary holiness," which is intended to designate the exemplary character of these women. The first Christian communities admired their strength of faith, their unconquerable hope and humility.

Of this they give a shining example at all times, without pre-
judice to many an imperfection.

6a. . . . *as Sarah obeyed Abraham, calling him lord. And you are*
now her children if you do right . . .

In the Old Testament there is, indeed, a passage in which Sarah
speaks of Abraham as her lord, but there is hardly any mention
of obedience: " So Sarah laughed to herself, saying, After I have
grown old, and my husband is old, shall I have pleasure? " (Gen.
18:12). Perhaps Peter is thinking of other late Jewish texts lost
to us now. After the Dead Sea findings we know that such
detailed accounts of the physical and spiritual merits of the
ancestral mother of the chosen people existed. In the case of
Christian women, who as " God-fearing " had already come into
contact with the Jewish religion, the wish to become the spiritual
children of Sarah is understandable. They probably thought of
the remarkable text which once the prophet declaimed to the
exiles in Babylon to console them: " Hearken to me, you who
pursue deliverance, you who seek the Lord; look to the rock
from which you were hewn, and to the quarry from which you
were digged. Look to Abram your father and to Sarah who bore
you " (Is. 51:1f.). Whoever is a child of Sarah is also a child of
Abram. Not empty words, indeed, not even circumcision could
truly secure this childhood. A Jewish text states: " Whoever has
pity on his fellow man is certain to belong to the seed of our
father Abram; but whoever has no pity on his fellow man is certain not to belong to the seed of our father Abram." Only that
love which arises out of a lively faith and is effective in the
strength of this faith can lead one into the community of those
children to which a centurion of Capharnaum, a Lazarus, or a
Zachaeus belong.

[6b]. . . *and let nothing terrify you.*

This final sentence contains the necessary conclusion of the entire exhortation. Previously the submission of the women was emphasized only from various points of view. Not till the conclusion here are strength and firmness added to the picture of the Christian woman. Sometimes the wife can be of a different opinion than her husband. The exhortation to let nothing terrify her does not necessarily have in mind the possibility of the heathen husband doing her an injustice or commanding her under threat to give up her faith. It is sufficient to think of the moody anger, the fury or the irritable rantings of a man which, of course, shake the female soul to its depths. Thinking of such family scenes Peter sympathetically indicates to women their greatness based on the divine, their power, and their free dignity. Their submission to the husband ought not to arise from a timid fearfulness or slavish subservience. They were ransomed by the death of Christ and are therefore truly free. The woman accepts through free love for God the natural order of creation and is submissive to her husband. However, submission as the " handmaid of the Lord " (Lk. 1 : 38) means in last analysis an exaltation. In conclusion, then, the whole symmetrical portrait of the Christian wife, presented in this section, is shown. Its characteristic features are humble submission, peace-loving beneficence, and freedom from fear of others as fruit of the loving fear of God.

The Duties of Husbands (3 : 7)

THE EXHORTATION (3 : 7a)

[7a]*Likewise you husbands, live considerately with your wives, bestowing honor on the woman as the weaker sex . . .*

While all Christians have been exhorted to be submissive to the state (2:13), the servants to their masters (2:18), and the wives to their husbands (3:1), the exhortation for men asks them to be considerate to their wives. They are to consider the value which their wives have in the eyes of God and should honor them accordingly. Wives and mothers are for Peter human beings who resemble the suffering Lord in many ways. Because of the physical and spiritual sufferings which they bear in silence God looks down on them with special favor. They are in his grace. Precisely because of their weakness they become, seen with the eyes of faith, great.

Peter exhorts men to change from their heathen standards to a Christian assessment of their life's-companion. Also from these " house-masters " does he demand some of the Christian foolishness of the cross. It is the same foolishness which urges slaves to suffer undeservedly and housewives to give in quietly when opinions differ. Peter believes men to be capable of such an attitude which responds precisely to such weaker and needy women and " chivalrously " accepts them.

THE FIRST REASON: THE DIGNITY OF WOMEN (3:7b)

7b. . . since you are joint heirs of the grace of life . . .

Husbands are confronted with the rightful viewpoint: Your wives will in eternity be equal " joint heirs " of Christ (Rom. 8:17). Already in 1:4 the future " inheritance which is imperishable, undefiled, and unfading " was described in such glowing terms: the fullness of life of the body-soul personality united to Christ in the community of saints. " In the resurrection they neither marry nor are given in marriage, but are like angels in heaven " (Mt. 22:30). This evaluation of women was an unheard of novelty in those days. Thus the apostolic teaching concerning the finally valid relationship between married partners is expressed in a few simple words.

THE SECOND REASON: THAT PRAYER BE UNHINDERED (3:7c)

7c. . . in order that your prayers may not be hindered.

Peter imagines prayer to be something which has to travel in order to get to God. The prayers of men—communal prayer is not explicitly mentioned—could as it were be hindered on this journey if they had been inconsiderate to their wives. Not only prayers of petition are implied here, in which cases the anxiety to be heard would be most comprehensible. For Peter, prayer means the intercourse between man and God, the most important task in the spiritual life of the Christian. In 4:7 there will be mention of the need for inner quiet and sobriety as the best preparation for prayer. A Christian who can no longer pray effectively misses his chief task. So we can understand why the directive concerning the hindrance of prayer forms the final argument in the exhortation of men. All other activities of the weekday must be directed towards prayer. Suddenly such barely noticeable everyday things as inconsiderateness or lovelessness in the circle of the family become hindrances which put the most essential thing into jeopardy.

Final Exhortation of Responsibilities (3:8-12)

8Finally, all of you, have unity of spirit, sympathy, love of the brethren, a tender heart and a humble mind.

What a wonderful catalog of all those spiritual and ethical traits which a Christian must possess as a member of the church, as a building stone (2:5) which fits into, and supports the structure. At the same time ascetical directives are given. All these " virtues " are for the sake of the community without being exhausted, as often happens nowadays, by purely natural motives. This becomes clear in the word humble. To have " the mind of a servant " only becomes comprehensible through a belief in Christ. For to the world of that time the humble, " lowly thinking " mentality was regarded as weakness—as it generally is today. The term " slave-morality of Christianity " still rings in our ears. Only the strong, the noble, the vital which has conquered all weakness seems to be of value. Here, however, values are truly " revalued " when we have " unity of spirit, sympathy, love of the brethren, a tender heart, and a humble mind."

⁹Do not return evil for evil, or reviling for reviling; but on the contrary bless, for to this you have been called, that you may obtain a blessing.

These exhortations to be good-natured and to bear injustice gladly sound like an application of the Sermon on the Mount to the weekday: " You, therefore, must be perfect, as your heavenly Father is perfect " (Mt. 5:48). All these demands to repay evil with good bind every Christian. Jesus did not preach a utopian ideal. In keeping with the circumstances every hearer or reader of the letter ought to act within his environment not in accordance with the letter but with the spirit of the Sermon on the Mount. It is not recommended that one should timidly yield in matters of principle. This has become clear many times in the letter so far (2:16; 3:6). People who draw their strength from a fellowship with Christ, in final analysis, do not find it necessary to insist on their personal "honor" or their "good name." They rather possess the courage to forgive even vituperative and unjust critics. The climax of this forgiveness is the positive conferring of the blessing of God in keeping with the Lord's commandment: "Love your enemies, do good to those who hate you, bless those who curse you, pray for those who abuse you" (Lk. 6:27f.).

The Greek word "to bless" means first of all "to call good." A Christian who "blesses" like that has discovered something good in the other and likes to speak of it. He wishes him good also in cases where there is no immediately discernible justification for this good will. The true reason is hidden. It is the benediction of God which has previously been given to this man who blesses and has presented him with that fullness of blessing (cf. 1:26) from which he only dispenses. God has pronounced "good" every man born anew in baptism, just as he once spoke over Adam before the fall that "everything is good" (Gen. 1:31). After the fall the situation changed. The human being was no longer pleasing to God without reservation. Not till God's Son became man and suffered did the condition change. Earlier on, it was said that Christians were called to suffer (2:21a); now it is said that they are called to possess the fullness of God's blessing. Whoever suffers in union with Christ is again in a special way pleasing to God (4:14), he is called "good," he possesses his grace and his blessing. From such a fullness of blessing the Christian can also, even in his environment, dispense priestly blessings. If in this he prefers to use the sign of the cross, then this has a deep significance.

[10]*For "He that would love life and see good days, let him keep*

his tongue from evil and his lips from speaking guile; [11]*let him turn away from evil and do right; let him seek peace and pursue it."*

Just as the section above on the spiritual exodus from Egypt (1:13—2:10) was concluded with a quotation from the Bible, even so do the exhortations of the "catalog of duties" end in verses from the Old Testament. By means of the little word "for" the verses of the psalm are joined to the preceding verse on the fullness of blessing. Peter bestows this blessing upon the communities from his heart and confirms once more on what it is founded: on the virtues aimed at community life described above (3:8). When he speaks of "life" and "good days" he means one and the same thing, that life already basically glad upon earth (1:6) but flowing out into eternal rejoicing in heaven (4:13) which is the "inheritance" (3:9) of the Christian. By keeping the tongue and lips from evil one must not forget the unspoken words of the heart. Such unspoken words often embitter the life of people more than open conflict and hinder the blessing of God.

The image of "turning away from" once more conjures up the idea of the wanderer who finds himself on a "way of life" (1:13.15). But the image of the human being who pursues peace is new. The word "pursue" is otherwise used when there is talk of chasing after animals or fleeing enemies. Just so are all who are at peace to be concerned with unity and reconciliation. Whoever makes use of every possibility of reestablishing peace, with those who hold a grudge, pursues peace. Those Christians, who love peace and pursue it, will become peacemakers wherever they go and will, at the same time, find divine life and "good days" for themselves and their contemporaries. In the beatitudes of the Sermon on the Mount Jesus says: " Blessed are the peacemakers for they shall be called the sons of God " (Mt. 5:9). The pursuit of the good shall lead ever nearer to the absolutely good God and shall be crowned by his sonship.

[12]*For " the eyes of the Lord are upon the righteous, and his ears are open to their prayer. But the face of the Lord is against those that do evil."*

The righteous means those who " live to righteousness " (2:24) after the example of the representative suffering of Christ (2:24). On them rest with pleasure the " eyes of the Lord." Upon them he bestows a look of glad recognition while his angry face is turned towards those who are wilfully disobedient.

Scripture is full of anthropomorphic statements concerning God. This does not minimize God's greatness, but man becomes aware of his impotence to grasp God's essence in a manner appropriate to him. Since God's Son has become man, the anthropomorphic ideas concerning God receive a new justification. God's power, mercy, goodness, and patience became visible through the Incarnation of the eternal Word. Not only by virtue of his divine nature, but also insofar as he is a whole man Christ could say to Philip: " He who has seen me, has seen the Father " (Jn. 14:9).

Also God's eyes have become more easy to imagine through the so often described look of Christ in the New Testament. When Andrew for the first time on the Jordan led his brother Simon to the Lord, " Jesus looked at him " (Jn. 1:42). This first look remained unforgettable for Peter just as did the look after the denial in the courtyard of the high priest when in passing the Lord " turned and looked at Peter " (Lk. 22:61). And in the

case of the rich youth, " Jesus looking upon him, loved him "
(Mk. 10: 21). When a Christian has discovered favor in the " eyes
of God " his enthusiasm to live a life pleasing to God is fanned
anew. The whole letter could also be understood to be a letter on
the joy which lies in finding grace in the eyes of God. The
knowledge that the eyes of God constantly rest on the one who
fears God, is a great consolation, as is the security that he also
sees all the good, hidden to the eyes of men, which such a person
does.

Exhortation to Remain Faithful in Persecution (3:13–22)

In the verses, quoted from the psalms, good people were set in
opposition to people who " do evil " (3: 12b). Peter interrupts the
verse from the psalm and joins the idea " to do evil " to the
related one " to harm you " (3: 13a). He thinks it hardly possible that people exist who would maliciously harm Christians
who do their duty. All summonses and persecutions of Christians
arise more from ignorance of the true nature of Christianity
than from malice. Therefore it is proper, courageously and in-
trepidly, to give a defense of the Christian faith after the example of Christ and in fidelity to the baptismal promises.

In Persecution Tell of the Hope Within You (3 : 13–17)

A BASIC OBJECTION (3:13)

13Now who is there to harm you if you are zealous for what is
right?

To a healthy piety which lives through hope there belongs zeal
for what is good, zealousness in doing good works, in putting
into action the exhortations just given (2:11—3:12). Like men-
ials, ready to be of service—for, indeed, we are "servants of
God" (2:16)—we are to "pursue peace" (3:11), to exert ourselves "earnestly" to show love to others (1:22; 4:8), to practice hospitality "ungrudgingly" (4:9). Such zeal will only then
turn into jealousy if someone, exerting himself on the path to
God, forgets that all seeming actions of his own have become
possible only through God-given gifts (cf. 4:11); if he no longer
keeps in mind that he works with "talents" which God has lent
him (cf. Mt. 25:15).

Be Ready to Make a Courageous Stand (3:14–15)

[14a]*But even if you do suffer for righteousness' sake, you will be
blessed.*

Suffering is not only an occasionally unavoidable evil, but an
excellent opportunity to live a Christian life. We almost hear a
note of secret joy, not forgetting, of course, that suffering will
always be suffering. This note is struck in a surprise benediction.
Only once more does this "blessed" appear in our letter: "If
you are reproached for the name of Christ, you are blessed"
(4:14). The same "blessed" is repeated in the Sermon on the
Mount nine times. There the benediction, for those who suffer
persecution falsely, marks the end of the beatitudes. The rejoicing of those passages is also here audible: "Blessed are those
who are persecuted for righteousness' sake, for theirs is the kingdom of heaven. Rejoice and be glad, for your reward is great in

heaven " (Mt. 5:10.12a). For Peter the obvious fruit of a life of righteousness is, to be sure, an undisturbed peace (3:13). As a second, even more valuable fruit, he names the suffering of persecution. The high-minded spirit of martyrdom of this letter, nourished by a lively faith, breaks through radiantly.

[14b]*Have no fear of them, nor be troubled,* [15a]*but in your heart reverence Christ as Lord.*

Peter expresses his thoughts in words which he is familiar with from the prophet Isaiah. In three seemingly trivial points he diverges, however, from the original. They throw a light on the manner in which the earliest Christians meditated on the scriptures, that is, on the scriptural readings of the young church.

Peter was confronted with a text in which the prophet exhorts the God-fearing not to dread the attack of the enemy army, specifically that of the king of Assyria: " And do not fear what they fear, nor be in dread. But the Lord of hosts him you shall regard as holy; let him be your fear " (Is. 8:12f.). First of all " what they fear," that is to say, the king of Assyria, is changed into " them." This transposes the significance of the passage from the past into the present situation. On the basis of the verses which follow, " them " may well refer to official courts, judges, or also torturers who played such a large role in Roman justice. Secondly, " the Lord of hosts " is changed into Christ as Lord. Everything that is said in the Old Testament concerning Yahweh, the Lord of hosts, applies also to the Trinity and therefore also to Christ. Finally, the passage from the prophet says: " Him you shall regard as holy; let him be your fear." While God in Is. 6:3, as the three times holy One, stands at a distance unapproachable and awful, he has now come near to humanity.

He has " dwelt among us " (Jn. 1:14). Therefore this Lord is to be regarded as holy quite personally in one's heart and to be adored there. In him they are to find the strength to stand up fearlessly as martyrs, as witnesses to the truth even before emperors.

15b*Always be prepared to make a defense to any one who calls you to account for the hope that is in you . . .*

During interrogations the faith is not to be kept a secret through fear. Not only can a defense be demanded of Christianity, it can also be given. One can demonstrate that it is reasonable to live a Christian life. That does not say that others will also believe after such a demonstration. For this, God's grace, his " visitation " (2:12), would be necessary. Above all, hope is to be defended, because it gives meaning to one's whole life—present and future.

Is not the hope of eternal life precisely that which is most alien to all natural explanations? The apostles were of a different opinion. They were convinced that every human being who is not prejudiced must acknowledge the arguments which can be cited for the bodily resurrection of Christ from the dead. If Christ has risen from the dead, why should it be unreasonable that his followers also live in the hope of a resurrection? " If for this life only we have hoped in Christ, we are of all men most to be pitied " (1 Cor. 15:19).

ALWAYS DO IT WITH GENTLENESS AND REVERENCE (3:16)

16*. . . yet do it with gentleness and reverence; and keep your*

conscience clear, so that when you are abused, those who revile
your good behavior in Christ may be put to shame.

Standing before the judge is also missionary work. Never should
the reverence due to a representative of the state (2:17) be forgotten. Indeed, one should believe in the essential goodness of
these people and approach them with benevolence. Christ acted
thus when he took Pontius Pilate seriously in spite of his injustice and fear of men and treated his questions and doubts with
gentleness. The whole verse makes one think of the happenings
at the praetorium in Jerusalem: outside the people are shouting
that Jesus is an agitator and an enemy of the emperor. But the
regal composure and patience with which the accused stands
before his judge is a judgment on the lies of the accusers. Christians should stand before their accusers and judges in Christ,
that is to say, like Christ and in union with him. They are to
contemplate the life and death of Christ. Indeed, they have been
drawn into that occurrence which is Christ. In them Christ
stands before the judge anew.

SUMMING UP: THE WILL OF GOD (3:17)

[17]*For it is better to suffer for doing right, if that should be God's*
will, than for doing wrong.

He who truthfully attempts to live a Christian life, will also
want to become like Christ in his Yes to the will of the Father.
With a fine tact Peter shows how much understanding he has
of the difficulties and distress which a persecution brings to the
community. He seems fairly to wrestle with a form in which to

express, as sparingly as possible, this possibility of God-sent trials which must be reckoned with. He knows that this wish of God to go in the way of the cross is not always easy to fulfill. And yet the deepest consolation for the tried Christians will lie in the certainty that it is the will of the Father. To suffer persecution in accordance with God's will and for the sake of righteousness is something different from standing in court because of a criminal offense. Peter knows that often the worst trial is to be equated with the criminal in the public opinion and to be branded an enemy of the people. But they should use this situation also to proclaim Christ (3 : 15b). They are, however, to find their consolation and strength in the knowledge: Nothing happens without the Father willing it.

Christ's Example and the Baptismal Promises (3 : 18-22)

CHRIST'S EXAMPLE AS A SACRIFICE FOR SIN (3 : 18)

[18a]*For Christ also died for sins once for all, the righteous for the unrighteous, that he might bring us to God . . .*

Again (as in 2 : 21-25) the portrait of the crucified is painted with the colors of the prophet Isaiah. The death of the Lord on the cross was an offering for sin: " Yet it was the will of the Lord to bruise him; he has put him to grief; when he makes himself an offering for sin, he shall see his offspring, he shall prolong his days " (Is. 53 : 10). Like Christ, his disciples, who might in the nearest future stand before a judge as accused and hear their death sentence, should be ready to place their lives as an offering for the sins of others into the scale of God's justice . . . So they

too will " bring people to God " or—in the words of Isaiah—
they shall " see their offspring."

¹⁸ᵇ. . . *being put to death in the flesh but made alive in the*
spirit . . .

Once more an aspect of the passion is highlighted which delivers
a message to those who must reckon with the possibility of being
condemned to death: it was precisely in death that the greatest
activity of Christ began. The body trembled, became weak and
bled to death. In the sphere of the spirit, however, the earthly
execution of Christ began to work and " draw all men to himself " (Jn. 12:32). Those Christians in Asia Minor who are
troubled as to who will take over their work once they have
been eliminated because of their uncompromising attitude are
told that then they can be even more active since for them death
means being made alive in the spirit. The young church knew
from experience of the power which emanates from men who die
in Christ. Those who died in this way often converted men who
were entirely unapproachable before.

Christ as Preacher of Martyrdom (3:19-20)

¹⁹. . . *in which he went and preached to the spirits in prison . . .*

The lively spiritual effectiveness of Jesus, which began with his
death and so can be an example for the martyrs, is highlighted
by the preaching of his victorious death " in prison." In keeping
with the conviction of the young church Christ was active in the
underworld during the hours which passed between his death

and his resurrection. The happening in this intermediary time is portrayed by Peter in pictures taken from the imaginative world of late Judaism. The " prison " is to be understood as a place in the earth's interior where the fallen spirits are held captive, a place of punishment and horror. The Book of Henoch tells also of a task which was imposed on Henoch: " Henoch, thou writer of righteousness, go and announce to the (fallen) keepers of heaven . . ." Christ went down to this place to give an account of himself and his death—whether to their salvation or to their judgment one cannot tell from this passage. A double truth was to be expressed with this image: The act of salvation of the Lord was an occurrence which involved all domains of the world and actualized the judgment and grace of God. And furthermore: Christ is the faithful witness, the martyr who preaches it to all beings after his saving act—even to those at enmity with God. Just so he wishes that he be preached through us everywhere and at all times . . .

²⁰. . . who formerly did not obey, when God's patience waited in the days of Noah . . .

The idea of preaching is developed further. Peter moves from the idea of spirits in general to particular disobedient people. Thereby two epochs in the history of salvation are conjured up, in which, in both instances, . " God's patience " waited before judgment: the time before the flood and the final period of Christianity. These two periods correspond to two groups of " disobedient " people who are preached to. At the time of the flood it was the people who ate and drank and fornicated while the evil of the fallen world of spirits stood behind them. At the time of the apostles it is the representatives of the heathen, ungodly state behind whom stand the satanic powers as the actual driving force. The Christians tremble at the thought of having to stand before such heathen judges (3:14b f.). But a new light is thrown on the situation by a glance into earlier history. As it did in those days the rational world now stands to be judged (4:7.17). The possibility still exists for many to be converted, but for the God-fearing there is the duty of preaching. Formerly, Noah, " a herald of righteousness (2 Pet, 2:5), performed this duty, then Christ, as the true Noah and as the true Henoch (3:19). Christians also have the duty of propagating God's justice by their fidelity even unto death. It seems as if God looks at their lives of righteousness and fear of God with indifference. In reality he wants, in accordance with his unfathomable decree, to give all people the possibility of making an explicit decision either for or against him, in fact, he almost forces them to do so (cf. 4:5).

[20b]. . . *during the building of the ark, in which a few, that is, eight persons, were saved through water.*

Even more clearly does the similarity between the prototype and the reality, in which the communities live, emerge. In those days everything was threatened with destruction in the floods of God's anger. But a means of salvation was kept ready, an ark, a box made of wood. The words indicate that this is more than a report of past occurrences: " build " signifies a creation in accordance with an artistic and wise plan, and means more than simply " to produce." Out of the material carpentry a spiritual furnishing emerges.

Moreover, it strikes one that the number of people is recorded because the number " eight " is, evidently, significant. As the completion of the seven-day week, this number has become a

symbol of everlasting duration; in Christianity the eighth day is
the commemoration day for the resurrection of the Lord. Circumcision, which was the preliminary step to Christian baptism,
took place on the eighth day; the baptismal font of the early
Christians was octagonal.

The suggestion of baptism becomes still clearer through the
words " through water." Noah could at most have been rescued
from the water or *over* the water. Only in view of baptism can
one validly say that souls are saved *through* water. Water is the
saving means through which Christians were led to the wood
and became dependent on the wood. So we come back to the
" ark." It is not intended here to be a symbol of the church, but
rather of the saving wood of the cross (cf. 2:24). Just as Noah, in
obedience to the Lord, entrusted himself during the flood to that
wood, just so shall our lives be united to the saving wood of the
cross, through water and the readiness to obey.

The Meaning of Baptism (3:21)

[21]*Baptism, which corresponds to this, now saves you, not as a
removal of dirt from the body but as an appeal to God for a
clear conscience, through the resurrection of Jesus Christ . . .*

What could so far be only inferred from hints, Peter now expresses clearly. He is not concerned with the occurrences in the
time of Noah, but with the occurrence of baptism. It is not the
external similarity—the use of water—that is decisive, but the
internal: here as there people subjected themselves unreservedly
to God in obedience. Baptism is above all a promise to God, a
concluded agreement. In the Letter to the Romans (6:17) it is

stated that the baptized person enters on a new relationship of
bondage: " you who were once slaves of sin have become
obedient from the heart to the standard of teaching to which
you were committed . . ."

Among the duties which Christians accepted at their baptism
the one which is now most opportune is brought into prominence: their promise to recognize God's holy will in all things,
to surrender themselves to him—and therefore to be also submissive to earthly judges (cf. 3:16).

The Example of the Victorious Christ (3:22)

22. . . . *who has gone into heaven and is at the right hand of God,*
with angels, authorities and powers subject to him.

First, Christ was portrayed as one who subjected himself to
earthly judges, who freely went to his death and who used his
death to propagate God's act of salvation. Now his image as
the victoriously enthroned king, whose " footstool " is made of
conquered enemies (Ps. 110 [109]:1) emerges. Now they are
completely subject to him. These subjects are more closely
identified by three names. Similar passages in the New Testament show that all three names are to be understood as inimical
to God. The word " authorities " means first and foremost
political authorities. In scripture invisible demonic powers often
fuse with visible political powers into one single great power. It
is the great ones of this earth, behind whom the power of Satan
stands, who now make Christians tremble. It is to their consolation that since Easterday Christ has triumphed over these
powers. Thus these verses, which show the Lord as an encourag-

ing example, harmonize with the basic note which had already
been struck at the beginning: " Have no fear of them nor be
troubled " (3:14).

Exhortation to Remain Firm in Temptation (4:1-6)

We are still within the second main part of the letter which
began in 2:11 with the address " Beloved." The theme of this
section was outlined in two verses (2:11f.): " Abstention from
the passions of the flesh " and " Good conduct among gentiles."
After the second theme has been developed, Peter once more
returns to the first in 4:1, that is, personal abstention in the
contest.

The Exhortation (4:1-2)

[1a]*Since therefore Christ suffered in the flesh, arm yourself with
the same thought . . .*

In 2:11 it was stated that the passions of the flesh· " wage war
against the soul." This world is a battlefield. The arms are of
prime importance for the outcome of every battle. In the Letter
to the Ephesians the apostle enumerates the " whole armor of
God " (Eph. 6:11). Truth is the girdle, righteousness is the
breastplate. The feet are shod " with the equipment of the
gospel of peace." Faith serves as a shield, salvation as a helmet,
and the word of God as " the sword of the spirit." The author
also speaks more . generally of the offensive and defensive
weapons " of righteousness " (2 Cor. 6:7) and exhorts us to put
on " the armor of light " (Rom. 13:12).

Peter is once again more prosaic and simple: The communities are to arm themselves with the inner disposition of, with the "thought" of, Christ. This thought was that he has taken on flesh in order "to learn obedience" (Heb. 5:8) by suffering in the flesh. The best weapon in the battle for salvation and life is the imitation of Christ in his willingness to suffer and carry the cross in accordance with God's will.

[1b]. . . *for whoever has suffered in the flesh has ceased from sin,* [2]*so as to live for the rest of the time in the flesh no longer by human passions but by the will of God.*

Peter means that suffering in the flesh which—sent by God—is freely affirmed and willingly accepted. Such a disposition not only saves one's soul, but also strengthens it. A human being who has penetrated the mystery of the cross has already ceased to sin. His attempt to "arm" himself with the thought of Christ means inner progress.

Put concretely, the loving imitation of the Lord made flesh consists of actualizing the will of God in one's life. It is that will which was the invigorating "food" of Jesus (Jn. 4:34). This one will also gives a great inner peace in times of distress, a peace which stands in opposition to the many earthly wishes, fears, and cares, and to "human passions." The singular mystery, which lies in one's appropriation of Christ's way of thinking, is that a seemingly heavy "yoke" (Mt. 11:29) gives rest, refreshment, and strength to one's soul.

A Glance Back Into the Past (4: 3)

[3]*Let the time that is past suffice for doing what the gentiles like*

to do, living in licentiousness, passions, drunkenness, revels,
carousing, and lawless idolatry.

A note of bitterness is struck with the word " suffice." Looking
at the preceding and following verse one does not get the impression that such vices had been completely eradicated since
baptism in those communities. In spite of this no direct exhortation is given. The Apostle speaks of these vices as lying in the
past. Moreover, he accepts the excuse that they were influenced
by their environment: It was more through thoughtlessness that
they sinned than through freely willing to do " what the gentiles
like." This former involuntary conformity was exactly the
opposite to their present Yes to God's will which springs from
a free decision . . .

People who pander to vices always have the wish to persuade
others to join in, and they abuse the so-called " spoilsports."
This was doubly true in times when public life and earnings
were oriented towards officially permitted vices. It suffices to
mention the splendid brothel cased with marble excavated at
Ephesus, the bawdy-houses on the acropolis at Corinth, or the
theatrical life in the Rome of the Caesars. Peter paints a tragic
picture from the " previous history " of the baptized. But they
are the same people which he had regarded as the true Israel
($1:13$—$2:10$), and had addressed as a " chosen race," a " royal
priesthood " ($2:9$). How great a faith and daring is needed to
hold so unflinchingly fast to one's aim.

Unworldliness Evokes Surprise and Abuse (4:4)

[4]*They are surprised that you do not now join them in the same*
wild profligacy, and they abuse you . . .

It is that surprise which the world shows when something of the divine reality breaks in on its habitual environment, which is at issue here. What seemed so natural is now suddenly regarded by some as vice. Indeed, they do not speak about these things, but neither do they any longer join in. And this is looked on as a reproach. It does not let them rest. Why not? At first persuasive words are used, but when these do not work the mood changes into hate and mockery against the " outsider." We know from non-Christian sources what a sensation Christians caused even in the first century by their new style of life. Their sober way of being pious (cf. 4:7b) is essentially different from that of any other religion. Much of it fell like a foreign body in society, yet some non-Christians must have felt that there was something right, reasonable, and worthy of human regard in their behavior.

Prospect of the Final Judgment (4:5-6)

5 *. . . but they will give account to him who is ready to judge the living and the dead.*

Also people who have heard little or nothing about Christ will have Christ as judge. When they laughed at those who wanted to live " righteously," they set themselves in opposition to Christ, for wherever the righteous suffer there Christ suffers. Peter is convinced that all those mockers knew in their conscience what is right and what is wrong. Christ is the universally valid moral yardstick for humanity and thereby its sole judge. Jesus says: " The Father judges no one, but has given all judgment to the

Son " (Jn. 5:22). Neither the living nor those who had died before shall be excluded from his judgment. It was Peter who announced Christ as this judge before the centurion Cornelius. Thereby he appealed to a command of the Lord: " And he commanded us to preach to the people, and to testify that he is the one ordained by God to be the judge of the living and the dead " (Acts 10:42).

⁶For this is why the gospel was preached even to the dead, that though judged in the flesh like men, they might live in the spirit like God.

How then can the gospel be preached to the dead of past centuries? The word " gospel " in a non-biblical, linguistic usage meant a messenger bringing through the realm the news of the coronation of a new monarch or the outcome of a decisive battle. Such news means joy and salvation for the friends of the new king, but for his enemies fear and punishment. Similarly, the preaching of the Christian " gospel " is news of a spiritual victory and an eternal accession to a throne. Although it actually means " good tidings " it also proclaims the judgment of God's enemies.

Peter speaks of this reality. Through Christ and his death out of love for humanity there becomes recognizable with a final clarity to the still living and long dead what is good and what is evil. The cross becomes the touchstone in the judgment on the " living and dead." For some this cross means eternal pain, for others eternal life in the contemplation of God: " The dead will hear the voice of the Son of God . . . and come forth, those who have done good, to the resurrection of life, and those who have done evil, to the resurrection of judgment " (Jn. 5:25-29).

Concluding Exhortations for Community Life (4:7-11)

The verses 4:8–11 sum up the thoughts so far and present the most important concern: the exhortation to Christians to love one another.

You Stand at the End of All Things (4 : 7)

⁷ᵃ*The end of all things is at hand . . .*

When in other places there is talk of the end of the world one easily senses a mood of timidity and resignation. For Peter the end of all things is a great occurrence which is awaited with trembling, joy, and fear. One faces it as the " outcome of faith " (1:9). The exhortations in Peter's letter already had this end in mind; the whole letter is sustained by a basic attitude which is only now named: Christian time is the end of time, Christians stand in " the last hour " (1 Jn. 2:18). Already the passage concerning the " chosen ones " (1:1) pointed in this direction. Peter can announce to the communities that the ardently wanted epoch of human history has dawned.

With it, however, the great judgment is at hand. This knowledge is serious (4:17) and joyful (1:6; 4:13) at the same time, for judgment has not only a negative side in condemnation, but also a positive side in the reestablishment of the just, God-willed order. The Christian awaits the Lord in the years of his earthly life as he might await a sovereign who is about to enter a city to establish justice. This royal procession is approaching nearer and

nearer, and, with James, Peter would like to call to us: " You
also be patient. Establish your hearts; for the coming of the Lord
is at hand " (Jas. 5 : 8).

7b. . . therefore keep sane and sober for your prayers.

Everything is now at stake to establish a relationship with the
other world which is approaching nearer and nearer. Prayer
becomes more and more important. Peter does not mean that
Christians are to pray to live sane and sober until the judgment
day; rather, they should be sane and sober in order to pray well.
Every good prayer, including communal liturgical prayer, demands preparation. Two types of preparations are mentioned,
and the third may be inferred accordingly. First, there is that
inner tranquillity which makes it possible for people to think
clearly. Spiritual and mental health is at stake. Besides health, it
is important also for good prayer that the soul be strengthened
by abstinence. This strengthening sobriety has already been mentioned (1 : 13). Later there is once more a cry for the conflict situation: " Be sober, be watchful " (5:8). This brings us to the
third presupposition for good prayer: spiritual watchfulness. To
remain spiritually watchful will only be possible to the sober.
Hence watchfulness and sobriety belong so closely together in
the teaching of the Apostle. Paul warns: " So then let us not
sleep, as others do, but let us keep awake and be sober " (1 Thess.
5:6). Sanity, sobriety, and watchfulness are the marks of a
Christian man of prayer. These are the characteristics which
Jesus so vividly illustrated in the parables of the ten virgins (Mt.
25:1–13), and of the men who, girded and with burning lamps,
awaited the bridegroom (Lk. 12:35–38).

Love One Another (4 : 8–9)

⁸*Above all hold unfailing your love for one another, since love
covers a multitude of sins.*

How is the thought, " love covers a multitude of sins," to be
understood? Does Peter exhort the Christian communities to a
mutual love because he wishes the faults of brothers and sisters
to be covered over and forgotten and no longer spoken of? Or is
love so important because God himself intervenes where Christians love one another? But whose sins does love cover? Those of
the beloved or of the lover?

Peter says: Whoever thinks of others and does them good
cares best of all for his own soul. The final judgment is at hand
—be it at death or at the end of the history of humanity. We are
to look back to our former life (4:3). Shall we be able to withstand the scrutiny of God's judgment? The Apostle recommends
what was for him the only thing capable of covering an earlier
failing and even to outshine it: love.

⁹*Practice hospitality ungrudgingly to one another.*

Evidently there were some Christians even in the young church
who complained of the burden laid on them by fellow Christian
travelers. Such grudging hospitality did not seem to be entirely
without foundation. Already at the end of the first century it
became necessary to give directives, not only on how Christian
hospitality should be offered but also on how it should be accepted. Hosts should receive a messenger of the faith " as if it
were the Lord." The guest, however, " should remain only a

day, if necessary a second day. If, however, he remains three days he is a prophet of lies." Many texts of the Old and New Testaments speak of that type of neighborly love which treats the traveling stranger as a friend. At the last judgment Christ will ask whether we had given shelter to " the least of his brethren " (Mt. 25 : 31–40). But there is no other passage which exhorts us to practice hospitality " ungrudgingly." What is at issue for Peter is the intention of the host. He looks with the eyes of faith at those who receive the traveling brother in Christ. A grudging reception would nullify a work of love; for God loves the willing and " cheerful giver " (2 Cor. 9 : 7).

Serve One Another For the Glory of God (4 : 10–11)

[10]*As each has received a gift, employ it for one another, as good stewards of God's varied grace . . .*

In the Letter to the Romans we are exhorted in a similar fashion to employ our various gifts for the good of the community. Paul uses the image of the body whose limbs must coöperate with one another (Rom. 12 : 3–8), whereas Peter remains faithful to his image of the house (cf. 2 : 5). In the church, the " household of God " (4 : 17), many stewards have their duties to perform. They must administer and apportion their master's property " faithfully and wisely " (Lk. 12 : 42). What was entrusted to them is " varied " or " motley." One can perhaps set to work in the fields with energy, another can teach and lead a community. The motley fullness of God's property is so great that no one has gone empty-handed. Each one has something to administer. Every servant has been entrusted with a duty by the Lord of the household, all talents are to be made use of. No one is worthless; even the smallest natural or supernatural talent is God's gift of grace.

[11]a. . . . *whoever speaks, as one who utters oracles of God; whoever renders service, as one who renders it by the strength which God supplies . . .*

Of the variety of God's gifts Peter gives prominence to two which are the most significant for the ministration of the communities: the ministry of the word, and serving tables (cf. Acts 6:2). The activities of lay-folk as well as the tasks of priests involve gifts which were entrusted to them by God. Therefore those who administer them should not only privately think of them as God's property. Rather, those who have received from them should be able to recognize that they have received from out of the treasure of God's gifts. One should be able to infer from the humble manner in which a person makes use of his psychological and spiritual, his physical and material powers for the sake of the community that he is aware of his duty of assisting others with these gifts. Above all those who are ministers of the word should give one the impression that they are not offering something of their own but are handing on God's gifts. Their speech should be animated by the same spirit as Jesus' when he said: "My teaching is not mine, but his who sent me . . . He who speaks on his own authority seeks his own glory" (Jn. 7:16.18).

[11]b. . . . *in order that in everything God may be glorified through Jesus Christ. To him belong glory and dominion for ever and ever. Amen.*

By means of this selfless, humble dispensation of the riches of

God, God is to be glorified. These concluding words refer not only to speaking and serving, not only to all other works of neighborly love within the church, mentioned in 4:8, but they are valid for all "good deeds," which was the subject of the exhortations of the main section. Peter returns here to a thought which he expressed at the start of this section: "Maintain good conduct among the gentiles so that . . . they may glorify God on the day of visitation" (2:12). God is to be glorified in that their fellow human beings should see Christians lead an upright and helpful life, especially in their day-to-day existence and in their dealings with one another. From this they are to become aware that another world and invisible values exist. Merely by recognizing this they already increase God's glory.

The entire letter is inspired by the thought of the eternal glory of God. Such a philosophy of life directed towards the glory of God is a continuation of the Old Testament inheritance. In a synagogue prayer we find: "Praise be to God that he has created us for his glory."

THE FINAL END OF THE CHRISTIAN
CALLING (4:12—5:11)

For the second time (cf. 2:11) Peter begins afresh with the address
"beloved." The main section (2:11—4:11) is finished. The third and
last part of the letter begins. The "amen" in 4:11 does not indicate
that this was the original end of the letter. What follows 4:11 is not
a later addition. In early Christian literature we often encounter such
a doxology in the middle of a letter—a doxology ending with
"amen," that is to say, "Yes, indeed, so it is and so it should be."

Peter once more takes up his basic thoughts and enlarges on them,
especially the concepts of purification (cf. 4:12 with 1:7), of suffering
with Christ (cf. 4:13 with 2:20f.), of good deeds (cf. 4:14–19 with
2:12), of judgment (cf. 4:17 with 4:7), of the flock of God (cf. 5:2–4
with 2:25), of submission (cf. 5:5f. with 2:13—3:6), and of eternal
glory (cf. 5:10 with 1:7).

Suffer in Union with Christ (4:12–19)

Rejoice to Share Christ's Sufferings (4:12–14)

¹²*Beloved, do not be surprised at the fiery ordeal which comes
upon you to prove you, as though something strange were happening to you.*

When this letter is being read at divine service, the " chosen
ones " are to evaluate the trials they have suffered differently
from before. The final part begins with this in mind. That suf-

91

fering should accompany the Christian on his journey through life is frankly a normal state of affairs. To be sure we are here concerned with an especially painful ordeal, a fiery ordeal. In 1:7 there was already a reference to the fires of purification to which God wished to expose the gold of their faith. This fire of purification does not only consist of public persecutions and injustices. It can also be fanned by personal temptations. But more decisive is that in the Apocalypse the destruction of the ungodly city of Babylon at the end of time is said to be by " fire " (Rev. 18:9.18). Hence in this whole section there is a suggestion not only of the fires of purification but also of the final fire and with it the final judgment. Since God himself is " a devouring fire " (Is. 33:14), individuals and all of humanity will be drawn further into this fire the nearer they approach God. Only what is genuine and truthful will be able to withstand the fiery ordeal of God.

[13]*But rejoice insofar as you share Christ's sufferings, that you may also rejoice and be glad when his glory is revealed.*

Peter asks us to rejoice at being allowed to share Christ's sufferings. He exhorts us to rejoice especially at this community of suffering. As you suffer joyfully with Christ so you will wax into his eternal joy. This is only possible if this community of suffering is basically a community of love, if it arises from a great, quite personal love " of our Lord Jesus Christ." In the transition from this to eternal life nothing essentially changes. The joyful community of love will only be intensified to the highest degree. We encounter here a hidden feature of the entire letter: Union with Christ in the love of friendship, and the burning desire to be like him for love, is what inflames Peter, and this is the state to which he wishes to lead all the " chosen strangers."

14If you are reproached for the name of Christ, you are blessed, because the spirit of glory and of God rests upon you.

We find two images here, and the more easily intelligible one reminds us of the baptism of Jesus in the Jordan. Through the descent of the Holy Spirit Christians become like the Messiah who humbled himself at his baptism. But the passage does not merely say that the " spirit of God " rests upon those reproached for the name of Christ, but that the " glory " rests upon them as well. Often the books of the Old Testament refer to the glory of God and his majesty, which had descended upon the assembly of Israel and had " filled the house of the Lord." The persecuted Christians are the true temple and the spiritual house of God (4:17). The glory of the Lord rests upon them with preference.

Peter shows great tact in that of all sufferings he only mentions being reproached for the name of Christ: it is especially painful. Spiritually this verse taken from everyday life stands very close to the seemingly other-worldly and idealized passage from the Sermon on the Mount: " Blessed are you when men revile you " (Mt. 5:11).

Suffer for the Sake of Righteousness (4:15–16)

15But let none of you suffer as a murderer, or a thief, or a wrong-doer, or a mischief-maker; 16yet if one suffers as a Christian, let him not be ashamed, but under that name let him glorify God.

The word Christian (*christianos*) only occurs three times in the

New Testament. The members of the community at Antioch were first called this about the year A.D. 40 (Acts 11:26). In the summer of A.D. 60 "christianos" is for King Agrippa II in Caesarea a self-evident and current title (Acts 26:28). Our letter contains the third reference. This "christianos" means "Christians" just as the followers of Herod might be called "Herodians." In keeping with the current attitude to the leader of the "party" concerned such a designation could be an honorable title or one of reproach. In the reports of the Roman writers Tacitus and Pliny we can recognize the legal position of which Peter is thinking: At court Christians are accused of nothing else except of being Christians. In this name and through this name, intimately united to the Christ, they are to "glorify God." In the first place they should give glory to God by an exemplary life. But now they are to honor him by being submissive while he "proves" (4:12) them. They are to count it as an honor to suffer insults in the name of Christ for he himself was also insulted.

Suffer Knowing that the Final Judgment is at Hand (4:17–19)

[17a]*For the time has come for judgment to begin with the household of God . . .*

The "because" of 4:14 had introduced the idea that God's glory and spirit rests with preference upon those who suffer. Here, as a second cause for being blessed, the passage continues that the time has come for judgment. As in the first argument, Peter sees the church here too as "the household of God," as a temple of God. The prophets have spoken about the beginning of judgment with the temple. Ezekiel reports in detail the begin-

ning of the divine judgment: God calls upon the powers, the
" executioners of the city." First, the priestly man " clothed in
linen " is to go through the middle of the city, through Jerusalem, and " put a mark upon the foreheads of the men who
sigh and groan at all the abominations that are committed in it."
They alone are to be spared. Then the command comes to
" ' Pass through the city after him and smite . . . And begin at
my sanctuary.' So they begin with the elders who were before
the house. Then he said to them, ' Defile the house, and fill the
courts with the slain. Go forth.' So they went forth and smote
in the city " (Ezek. 9: 1–7). It is the spectacle of a band of soldiers with drawn swords who rush first from the temple, through
the holy city and then upon the populace. This spectacle illus-
trates the necessity of a final purification, above all for the people
of God. One could use a different illustration: those who stand
before God to be judged are like the sick who await the surgeon
to perform a necessary and painful operation. Those patients who
are especially dear to the doctor he will take on first in spite of
the unavoidable pain. Saints like Catherine of Genoa, who regarded it as a grace to suffer already in this life and so to fore-
stall the purifying fire-torments of the next, have lived the truth
of this text.

*17band if it begins with us, what will be the end of those who do
not obey the gospel of God? 18And " If the righteous man is
scarcely saved, where will the impious and the sinner appear? "*

The exhortation to the righteous is emphasized by reminding
them of the fate of the impenitent sinner. The two interrogative
sentences underline the exhortations (4: 12–17a). The righteous
man is saved only " scarcely." This announces the great uncer-

tainty in which the Christian hovers during his time of battle on earth. Even Paul wrote to the Philippians that he had by no means reached the goal and that he must still " press on " for the prize (Phil. 3: 12–14). The seriousness of the situation is expressed by the words of the Lord whereby only the righteous who " endures to the end " will be saved (Mt. 24: 13). This " scarcely " also leads one to guess at the educational effort the heavenly Father has to expend to bring his children to the goal of perfection. The greatest effort, however, in " saving " us was expended by the Saviour, the Redeemer. " Wearied," Jesus once sat at the well of Jacob (Jn. 4: 6). He endured poverty, tiring work, wandering about year after year, homelessness, and finally death on the cross in order to save us.

[19]*Therefore let those who suffer according to God's will do right and entrust their souls to a faithful creator.*

God is the creator of the world, the sovereign, immutable maker and conserver, who remains faithful to himself. All anxieties and questions concerning suffering, which are repeatedly elucidated anew in this letter, are answered quite simply thereby: He is God the creator. He does not act senselessly.

When all considerations fail the thought of the creator and one's own creaturehood shall give the strength to endure distress. Yet endurance and sufferance are not inactive: we must press on doing right. This exhortation has resounded again and again. Often it became clearer by means of contrast to " those who do wrong," the evil-doers, what was at stake: the willingness to help and selfless love which become visible in good deeds in the circle of the family, in the community, and above all in public life. To do right is the ever constant duty without

regard to suffering or even to " the fiery ordeal." They are to
entrust their souls willingly to the creator for purification and
at the same time persevere in doing right. That is no easy task,
to entrust oneself always anew in faith to God. But Christ has
gone on this way before us (2:23) and became God's sacrificial
lamb. The life of a Christian will, through the continuously
repeated, uncompromising surrender of his own ego, to the
Creator, also become a sacrifice in the " fiery ordeal " of God.

Exhortation to God's Shepherds and Flock (5:1-5)

Exhortation to the Elders (5: 1-4)

*¹So I exhort the elders among you, as a fellow elder and witness
of the suffering of Christ, as well as a partaker in the glory that
is to be revealed.*

The letter is addressed to the community as such, to all its
members, as is demonstrated by the fact that the status of the
leaders must be given prominence by the words " among you."
Peter turns to the " elders " and calls himself, in brotherly
fellowship, a " fellow elder." To be an " elder " is to hold an
office and indicates a special priesthood outside the general
" holy priesthood " (2:5) of all Christians. The exhortation to
the elders is introduced by the little word " so." We have just
heard about doing one's duty in the weekday without regard
to suffering—and before that about the way in which suffering
and glory belong together (4:13). To this the Apostle adds:
So it will also be necessary for elders—for them especially—
to " do right " in the performance of daily duties, and to

combine with the hope of eternal glory the knowledge of the
necessity of the cross.

²ᵃ*Tend the flock of God that is your charge . . .*

The first word is significant for the spirit of the passage:
" tend." Peter himself received this task from the Lord: " Tend
my sheep " (Jn. 21:16). Similar thoughts are found in the
Old Testament: " To tend " includes royal government and
understanding leadership. He who tends the sheep must concern himself with grazing pasture and drink. He will give his
flock spiritual nourishment as Jesus did when he had com-
passion on the throng and taught them since they " were like
sheep without a shepherd " (Mk. 6:34). He will take special
care of the small and the weak and seek those who are lost.
Indeed, in keeping with the example of Christ he will be ready
to put his life at stake for his sheep. The shepherd is the head
of the flock on whom their well-being depends. A flock without
a shepherd will perish. It is all the more significant then that
the elders are urged to " tend the flock." Peter seems to be
conscious of his priorities. Does this " tend the flock " not
suggest, too, the later hierarchical structure of the church?

²ᵇ*. . . not by constraint but willingly as God would have you . . .*

The general obligation of tending the flock of God unfolds in
three separate exhortations. Each time the image of the bad
shepherd is contrasted with the image of the good shepherd.
The first admonition presupposes the official title " elders." To
be sure they were not constrained to take their office. But in the
course of their years of service the possibility of regarding this
office as a burden could well have arisen. The word " willingly "

indicates a glad fulfillment of duty which springs from one's own initiative. Such a willingness " as God would have it," is in accord with God if it is submissive to his will, takes note of his will, and unites itself with it. The Son of God willingly laid down " his life for his sheep " (Jn. 10:11).

^{2c}... *not for shameful gain but eagerly* ...

Perhaps " not for profit " would be a better translation of what is meant than the literal " not for shameful gain." Already in those days avarice at the expense of the community seemed to have been a vice of the clergy. The exhortation presupposes that the elders—we may perhaps compare them to our parish priests—received payment by salary or free contribution in accordance with the principle of the Lord: " the laborer deserves his food " (Mt. 10:10). Peter does not reject the payment to the elders by the community. He only objects to the desire for gain, the avarice of the clergy. When members of the community ask for service in the preaching of the gospel or the dispensation of the sacraments, the elders or clergy should be eager to comply without reference to payments or fees.

³... *not as domineering over those in your charge but being examples to the flock.*

Peter names a third aspect of the command to shepherds: " tend." The elders are not to reign over their charges like dictators. " Charge " represents the word " lot " which in the Old Testament means the land or possession which came to the tribes of Israel by lot as inheritance. But Israel itself was understood to be the " people and heritage " of God (Deut. 9:29).

Thus the Apostle warns the elders of a despotic rule over the communities, since they are not the allotment of the elders but God's possession and heritage.

There is an echo of a second meaning in these words, namely, the idea of rank. What is meant is the hierarchy of the clergy and the laity in the community which the individual has received by lot, either actually or figuratively. Looked at in this way, it is a warning against the self-glorifying and arbitrary changing and occupation of offices in the community. The " flock of God " is not to be unnecessarily disturbed.

The elders are to give their community an example of faithful fulfillment of duty. Like Christ they ought to be precursors (2:21) and leave behind their example to the flock, leave their " footsteps " (2:21) as the best exhortation. The leadership of the faithful through example demands the fulfillment of daily duties in all humility, keeping in mind the words of Jesus: " And whoever would be first among you must be slave of all " (Mk. 10:44).

4a*And when the chief shepherd is manifested . . .*

The title " chief shepherd " is a professional title. Such a chief shepherd obtains his assignments from a rich lord who is the owner of large flocks. Other shepherds, of whom he is the overseer, help him at his task. When Peter calls Christ the chief shepherd it means that he too is a shepherd together with the elders, but their chief. He will give assignments to his assistant shepherds or vicars and pay them their wages in accordance with their care for the flock. They must tend the flock of God which is at the same time his flock. When he returns he will see if his flock has grown, what returns it has made, how many animals

have been lost. The metaphor of the chief shepherd to whom
the Father " has given " the sheep (Jn. 10 : 29), who delegates to
others the task of " tending " the sheep (Jn. 21 : 16) together with
himself, throws light on the mystery of the apostolic succession.
What is most astonishing in God's plan of salvation is not so
much the fact that the office of shepherd was handed down
from the apostles to their successors, but that the Father handed
over to Christ and Christ to infirm human beings the task of
caring for " God's flock."

[4b]. . . *you will obtain the unfading crown of glory.*

The Apostle does not linger with the sober metaphor of a chief
shepherd who pays his assistant shepherds their wages, but
changes to the royal metaphor of a coronation. Wreath and
crown were synonyms in the ancient world. All that one could
imagine of joy, victory, and empire is contained in this. Peter
lets the shepherds, who are found faithful, hope for a crown of
unfading amaranths. This crown of dark-red blossoms becomes
a symbol of God's infinite glory of which they are to partake.
Eternal glory will be their reward and their prize of victory. So
the exhortation to the pastors and elders in this first pastoral
letter concludes with a prospect of eternal glory. All the failings
of the clergy, mentioned in 5 : 2f, seemed to be forgotten and a
high-spiritedness based on the power of the salvation of Christ
breaks through.

Exhortation to Those That Are "Younger" (5 : 5a)

[5a]*Likewise you that are younger be subject to the elders.*

To begin with, younger, like elder, does not refer to age but to
status in the ecclesiastical hierarchy. It is a title. Presumably
these " younger " ones were assistants and collaborators of the
community superiors and may be regarded as a first step in the
evolution of the later lower clergy. In the Acts of the Apostles
one finds for the first time such a service of assistance which
young men rendered in the management of the community :
" the young men " carried out the dead Ananias (Acts 5 : 6).
The subjection of the younger to the elder, which is so difficult
at all times, is seen by Peter through the eyes of faith. Thus it is
not a humiliation, but a possibility of realizing the first and
highest commandment, that of the love of God.

Exhortation to All (5 : 5b)

5bClothe yourselves, all of you, with humility towards one
another, for, " God opposes the proud, but gives grace to the
humble."

The fundamental reason why Peter so often and so emphatically
exhorts the recipients to be submissive is not that community
life might flow with less friction. The thought is decisive that
the humble person is pleasing to God and becomes like Christ.
He stands in the grace of God. In serving one another, especially
through humiliating work, the disciples grow in the imitation
of Christ, who came to atone for the pride of humanity by
obedient service. All, clerics and laymen, should put on humility
like clothing. Peter was perhaps thinking of the last evening
of Jesus, at the Last Supper: " . . . he rose from the supper,

laid aside his garments, and girded himself with a towel. Then he poured water into a basin and began to wash the disciples' feet, and to wipe them with the towel with which he was girded " (Jn. 13:5). That is the " example " (2:21) which all must imitate, those are the " footsteps " (2:21) in which all must follow.

Final Encouragement to Persevere (5: 6–11)

Trust in God (5: 6–7)

"Humble yourselves therefore under the mighty hand of God, that in due time he may exalt you.

The Apostle is thinking of a further type of humiliation. It receives its special tone through the metaphor of the mighty " hand of God." Persecutions have happened, others are near at hand. Peter counsels: Let yourselves be humiliated by human beings, who are only God's instruments, for thus you come under the power of God. God's judging, but also caring, power is his " mighty hand." The hand which is active and effective is the symbol of God's effective exercise of power. In the Old Testament, especially in connection with the exodus from Egypt, the hand of God, which is stronger than the " hand of the Egyptians," is repeatedly mentioned. " Thus the Lord saved Israel that day from the hand of the Egyptians and Israel saw the Egyptians dead upon the seashore. And Israel saw the great work which the Lord did against the Egyptians, and the people feared the Lord . . ." (Ex. 14:30f.). Under this strong hand

Christians are to suffer humiliation from the blows of fate. This hand of God will have the strength to set them up again. In the spirit and words of the letter the community of Lyon sent a report to Phrygia, in the year 177, that some among them achieved the crown of martyrdom with the mighty support of God: " Such distress the Christian churches had to bear under the above-mentioned emperor . . . They had humbled themselves under the strong hand of God, by which they now have been so magnificently exalted."

⁷Cast all your anxieties on him, for he cares about you

Like a burden which one loads on a pack-animal, the anxieties of Christians are to be cast on the heavenly Father. Surrounded by enemies, the psalmist gave himself courage with the words: " Cast your burden on the Lord, and he will sustain you; he will never permit the righteous to be moved " (Ps. 55[54] : 23). In all the sufferings of persecution God will not forget his communities. Indeed, no one will care about them as much as he. To be sure one cannot lay down regulations for him as to how he is to do this. Believing courageously, we must abandon ourselves to him.

Above (4 : 19), it was said that we are to persevere in doing right and leave the care of one's own person to God. " Casting off " one's own anxieties does not exclude our caring for other people, since we attempt to " do right " on their behalf. Thus the first communities understood the not so easy words of the Lord: " Therefore I tell you do not be anxious . . . But seek first his kingdom and his righteousness " (cf. Mt. 6 : 25–34). We are to be as a child to the heavenly Father, untroubled at our own future, only anxious to please the Father by obedience (cf. 1 : 14).

Be Watchful and Firm in Faith (5 : 8-9)

⁸Be sober, be watchful. Your adversary the devil prowls around like a roaring lion, seeking someone to devour.

Unexpectedly, the verse begins with a double, abrupt expression of alarm in extremity. The foundations of the faith are in danger. Are they all aware of what is at stake? Let us try to visualize the metaphor. When animals have been driven into a pen for the night, beasts of prey can do them no harm. A thick fence of stones and thornbushes surrounds them. But in the middle of the night the earth seems suddenly to tremble: near at hand, there is a roaring lion. The whole flock is set into panic. " The sheep run insanely against the thornbush, the goats cry out loud, the cattle with loud moans of fear rush together in wild groups, the camel tries to break its bonds in order to flee, and the courageous dogs who fight leopards and hyenas howl loudly and plaintively and flee whimpering in to the protection of their master." The lion roars at the sight of an animal preserve " with the intention of possibly making the pent-up animals blinded by fear break out."

This metaphor describes for Peter the coming development in Asia Minor. The enemies of the church of Christ, behind whom the power of the devil stands, will try to intimidate the faithful by threats. Entreating, the Apostle calls to them: Be sober. Recognize the situation for what it is. The lion is roaring to drive you into a helpless terror. He wants to frighten you so that you might break in confusion out of the flock and fold, which alone gives you protection, and run away. But when you have left Christ, his shepherds and his flock, then you are children of death.

⁹ᵃResist him, firm in your faith . . .

At the sight of the roaring lion the sheep of Christ are to stand firm, undisturbed. Through their faith they are to partake in the firmness of God. Their union with God is to give them the strength to remain in their place with composure, even when the powers of hell seem to break loose, when their enemies try to disquieten them by the severest threats and tortures.

True firmness can exist only where there is something unchanging and immutable. This is never the case in earthly things. God's trust, beauty, justice, and love will, however, never change; they shall remain eternally the same: Good shall for him be eternally good, and evil eternally evil. The " aliens and exiles " (2:11) already look to this quietness of eternity, the eternity of God. In courageous hope they have spiritually dropped anchor there, while the storm still rages and seeks to drive their ship loose. Their faith gives them strength to endure and remain firm, even in the dark night. One is not to prepare for the coming storm of slander and threats by organized action, but by patient resistance.

⁹ᵇ. . . knowing that the same experience of suffering is required of your brotherhood throughout the world.

This exhortation is followed by a short addition. Its intention is to console and encourage. You do not stand alone; the other communities throughout the world are in the same predicament. In the years 63–64 they have also been threatened with torture and death for persevering in Christianity. Besides this consoling thought one might also discern a modest implication that the senders of the letter in Rome, in this " Babylon " (5:13), have at least as much reason to become fearful. The Christians ought not to take their own troubles too seriously, but view them in the framework of the entire church. The view here extends from the individual communities to the entire church of Christ.

Here the church is not the " flock of God," nor the " household of God " and not the " body of Christ " but " the brotherhood." From the beginning Christians took over the custom of the Old Testament of calling one another " brother " and " sister." One saw an essential characteristic of the church in that it is a community of brothers who may call the same Lord " Father " (1:17); for through his living word alone new life has been given (1:3.23). In community, too, the children of God are educated, disciplined, and purified, precisely because he loves them. This painful process is now " required " of them for perfection: The scene of Christian life is laid at the end of time. Already the time has come when the judgment of God begins at the household of God (4:17). Brothers, separated in space but united in spirit, suffer in community as a " royal priesthood."

Prospect of Eternal Glory and Praise of God (5:10-11)

[10]*And after you have suffered a little while, the God of all grace, who has called you to his eternal glory in Christ, will himself restore, establish and strengthen you.* [11]*To him be the dominion for ever and ever. Amen.*
The great concern of courageous constancy is once more adopted.

The goal is " eternal glory," the irrevocable, victorious resurrection of the body. Three verbs follow which describe this psychophysical miracle of God, the resurrection of the body. The passage speaks of a triple action which God himself will undertake —this is expressly emphasized—on the faithful. To begin with it says God the Father will " restore " his children. Perhaps Peter was thinking of the restoration or the mending of damaged fishing nets (Mt. 4:21). In the case of bodies crushed by beasts of prey in the arena God will undertake a similarly difficult task. He will collect the bones as Ezekiel saw him doing in the scene of the great valley of death.

He will then also strengthen them so that vacillation and failure are no longer possible. What is now still the task of Peter, to " strengthen " the brethren in their faith (Lk. 22:32), will be taken over by the Father; instead of faith he will offer them vision. He will " invigorate " them, giving them the strength and energy of youth, he will refresh them like tired warriors on the " springs of living water " (Rev. 7:17; 21:1).

And, finally, he will " establish " this " spiritual house " of " living stones " (2:5), this " new Jerusalem " (Rev. 21:10), in his divine love. It will be possible then to say of these " aliens and exiles " in all truth: " being rooted and grounded in love, they may have power to comprehend with all the saints what is the breadth and length and height and depth " of God (Eph. 3:17f.).

THE CLOSE OF THE LETTER (5:12–14)

Whatever task Silvanus had in regard to the letter is not unam-
biguously revealed in the final remark of the letter. Silvanus
could be regarded as a collaborator in the composition of the
letter or as the bearer of it; both identifications seem to have been
the case. He is not recommended to the communities as a
"faithful brother" merely because he will conscientiously
deliver the letter. His character is illuminated and, moreover,
the Christians of Asia Minor are let know that they can depend
on the oral explanations which Silvanus might add to the short
letter.

Concluding Summary

[12a]*By Silvanus, a faithful brother as I regard him, I have written
briefly to you . . .*

Surprisingly, "as I regard him" is added. This addition has sense
only if it is an advantage to the bearer. This remark has such
value for a man like Silvanus only if the recipients are aware
who it is that stands behind this "private opinion"—a personality who in spite of collegial modesty (5:1) is well aware of his
leading position, who also knows that an opinion of his, expressed
merely as an aside, still has its weight in the communities. All
that is implied when we think of Peter as the "apostle of Jesus
Christ" (1:1).

[12b]. . . *exhorting and declaring that this is the true grace of God; stand fast in it.*

In a few words Peter expresses the contents of the entire letter. He wrote in order to " exhort " and to " declare." In the first place to exhort is mentioned. Peter wanted to urge the communities to have courage; he wanted to talk consolingly to them. Every line of the letter is inspired by the wish to encourage the faithful, just as a good shepherd might coax his sheep, urge them on, and cheer up those that are tired and want to remain behind by reminding them of the goal which the whole flock still must reach on the same day.

The second word, declare, here actually means: to corroborate testimony. Peter places himself with his authority behind the teachings of the messengers of the faith mentioned in 1:12 as " those who preached the good news to you." He declares them to be orthodox and testifies to the correctness of their teaching in the words wherein the cross and the hope in the resurrection took up a central position. Even in those days such a declaration was valued when made by that Apostle who lived in Rome and to whom the Lord had transferred his leadership.

Finally there is a last word on the true grace. All that has been said in the letter concerning grace is reawakened in the mind of the reader. One is to think especially of those passages which speak of suffering as a grace, that is, as a proof of God's favor and, at the same time, as a sorry condition. In this grace Christians are to stand fast, they are to have the courage to step into this in the beginning often painful favor of God, to stand fast in it and to stand it through all the blows of fate, to stand it out. In the insecurity of a time of persecution the Apostle sends words which are signposts: It is especially in suffering that you are true "Christians" pleasing to God (4:15). Be Christians gladly (4:13).

List of Greetings (5:13-14a)

¹³She who is at Babylon, who is likewise chosen, sends you greetings; and so does my son Mark. ¹⁴ᵃ*Greet one another with the kiss of love.*

The word "Babylon" leads our thoughts back to the introductory greeting (1:1). Recipients and sender live similarly in exile, that is to say, in a distant land, banished from the homeland. The community at Rome, as a spiritual, supernatural entity, sends greetings to the communities in Asia Minor. To this Peter adds a last exhortation springing from a heart full of caring love: The communities are to remain united in true love. In many passages of the New Testament there is a reference to a "holy kiss" with which Christians are to greet one another. But only Peter speaks of the "kiss of love." For him more is at issue than the kiss of peace at divine service. These words express his pastoral care and his feelings of responsibility for the harmony and unity of his entire flock, a unity not only due to his leadership, but also to mutual love. Already the flock is spread out "over the entire" (*kath' holon*) known world. It has already become truly "catholic." But it will not be sufficient if individual Christians in diverse places persevere in the right teaching till death. The visibly represented unity of the communities and groups of communities among themselves created by mutual love is to illuminate the essence of the church. For she is to be "one . . . so that the world may believe" (cf. Jn. 17:21) that this communion is not a human work but a reflection, even though weak, of divine love.

Signature of the Greeting (5:14b)

14b*Peace to all of you that are in Christ.*

The most beautiful paraphrase of the church can be read in the final greeting. She is the communion of people in Christ, the communion of all that suffer and are victorious in union with Christ. Two groups are addressed in these final words (assuredly in his own hand); the horizon widens while Peter is still writing. He wishes peace to a larger circle than the communities addressed so far. The passage does not say merely: Peace to all of you in Christ. But with generous open heart he includes also the many other communities of whom he has no definite news, but of whom he knows that they too will have to endure a similar battle, since they too follow Christ. Does he already surmise that his letter will soon be spread in copies all over the Roman empire?

Having from 4:12 onwards in the final part taken up again one theme after the other of the main part, having reminded us once more of the introduction (1:2) by the word " peace," Peter writes as the last word, emphatically placed at the end, a word which has dominated the entire letter: *Christ*. The wish to be like him, the contemplation of his example, and of his footsteps, the thought of his earthly sufferings and death, of his victory over the forces of evil, of his resurrection and enthronement on the right hand of the Father, were the forces which in this letter pressed on to further unfolding from verse to verse, which gave

it its fullness of life, its power to inspire, and that tone which
so often appealed to the reader personally. Perhaps this word,
which is here written in a clumsy fisherman's hand, is the most
beautiful expression of that mysterious unity of love which
exists between Christ, his representative and his flock since that
morning on the seashore when the words were exchanged:

—Simon, son of John, do you love me?

—Yes, Lord; you know that I love you.

—Tend my sheep (Jn. 21 : 16).

The Second Epistle
of Peter

INTRODUCTION

Conservation and Renewal

Our world is in a process of change. The church, if it is not to
back away from the confrontation with the world to which it
has been commissioned, cannot take up a position outside this
process. But how far can the church identify itself with this
process and not betray its own nature or renege on its divine
mission to the world? The author of the Second Epistle of Peter
was agitated by the same question. How did he solve the problem of remaining faithful to the faith handed down while taking
due cognizance of new initiatives?

Concessions to "novelty" were being made. Terms were
being used that seldom or never occur in biblical terminology.
They derived from Greek modes of thought and expression,
from a religious hunger that they were meant to still. Instead of
the faith, knowledge (gnosis) was spoken of; the consummation
of the Christian life in the final epoch was now referred to as
participation in the divine nature; moral conduct that corresponds to the will of God was not called righteousness but virtue.

But these "novelties" do not affect the essence of the Christian
proclamation. The faith remains the norm of orthodoxy. This
truth is the word of Christ in whom all revelation finds its
center; this word was proclaimed by the prophets and preached
to the New Testament community by the apostles. The new
expressions are only new vehicles of the traditional faith.

The Bible and Its Interpretation

In the dialogue between the church and the process of world change, sacred scripture has a special importance. It is not merely a container of divine revelation; it is itself the word of revelation and the first, if not the only, source of faith. For the author of the Second Epistle of Peter, the Bible is the book from which he teaches, reproves, and warns. He finds in it the defense of the truths of faith that are being questioned (1 : 16–21); he draws from it the facts of salvation history that are calculated to make one take thought (2 : 4–9); he finds in it the basis for his warnings. The Bible is the inspired word of God (1 : 21); it contains divine wisdom (3 : 15). The canon of holy scripture includes for him, besides the Old Testament writings, the gospels and the Pauline epistles.

But error also draws its proofs from sacred scripture. The Bible by itself is not enough; it requires interpretation and explanation. The fundamental rules of biblical interpretation are the following. The Bible is to be interpreted according to the Christ event, of which the apostles were eyewitnesses. The Bible can be rightly interpreted only by the man who has the Holy Spirit (1 : 21), and only he who confesses the Catholic teaching of faith handed down has the Spirit (cf. 1 Jn. 4 : 2). Interpretation must agree with the teaching of tradition. They who are not trained and imbued in the teaching of faith can easily give the Bible a false meaning (3 : 16).

Myth and Revelation

Can modern man, who accepts scientific thought, still believe in the Bible and therefore be a believer? The pastoral desire to save the Bible for the man of today has prompted some scholars to suggest that the Bible must be " demythologized," that myth must be excised from the sacred scriptures. What in the Bible is mythical? The three-storey picture of the world (heaven as the place of God, earth as the place of man, the nether world as the place of the dead); divine intervention in the world by miracles and prophecy; the incarnation, resurrection, ascension, and second coming of Christ. What remains of the Christian faith? Is it only a message to man that he is laid claim of from outside himself? Is it merely man's reflection on his inherent self-insufficiency? Where is the border between truth and myth?

This epistle must carry on debate with men who explain the coming of Christ as a human invention, a legend—or, as they put it, a " myth." They appeal to experience, they reason " scientifically." How are their arguments disproved? First the author meets the " scientific " theories half-way; he explains, as they, the end of the world by fire and the origin of the world from water. But he also makes it clear that he gives scientific theories a subordinate importance. The decisive factor in the genesis and end of the world is the Word of God that speaks the world into existence, destroys it, and creates it anew. The historicity of events for which there are eyewitnesses suggests a caution to outright surrender to demythologization. Christ will come in power and glory. This statement is credible because of the historical event of the transfiguration. History can be the criterion for deciding what is a figurative expression in the Bible and what is a literal truth that stands forever.

Law and Freedom

How reconcile the freedom of the sons of God, as proclaimed by St. Paul, and the obligation to observe the law and the many prescriptions laid down by the church? The man of today does not expect from religion new restrictions on his freedom, but rather its expansion. The Second Epistle of Peter envisages a similar situation: the freethinkers with whom the epistle must contend are convinced that they possess the divine Spirit, that they are sons of God, and that redemption has put them in a state of perfection. To what purpose then commandments and laws?

This problem raises radical questions concerning the Christian life. The Christian has already received the great blessing of redemption, but still he must exert himself to attain its final goal. He is free, and yet he still needs the " holy commandment." In baptism he was liberated from unruly passions, yet he must exercise a vigorous asceticism to avoid them. The law that binds the Christian is " the truth "—in the final analysis, it is Jesus Christ, Lord and redeemer, and the knowledge of the Lord. This knowledge includes both understanding and love. He who knows and loves the Lord does not need the law any longer, for he will do what the Lord reveals to him. But a plenary knowledge of the Lord is a blessing of salvation reserved to the last times.

The Christian life unfolds between the coming of Christ in weakness and ignominy and his coming in power and glory. The Christian already lives in the final era, but not all its aspects and implications have been revealed. Therefore, he needs the light of holy scripture. He must still grope in the darkness; his moral life is still effort and struggle against severe temptations. The Christian life can be rightly understood only if viewed in this tension between the first and second coming of Christ. Our freedom still needs the direction given by commandments.

OUTLINE

RESISTING NEW DOCTRINE (2:1—3:16)

I. False teaching on freedom (2:1–22)

  1. Liar-prophets (2:1–3)
    a) Against the Lord (2:1)
    b) Against the people of God (2:2–3)

  2. Just judgment (2:4–9)
    a) The punishment of the angels (2:4)
    b) The punishment by flood (2:5)
    c) The punishment of Sodom and Gomorrah (2:6–8)
    d) Twofold outcome (2:9–10a)

  3. Rooting out the false prophets (2:10b–14)
    a) Revilers (2:10b–12)
    b) Revelers (2:13–14)

  4. Fruitless frenzy (2:15–19)
    a) Veering from the right way (2:15–16)
    b) Desiccated springs (2:17–19)

  5. The final state (2:20–23)
    a) Relapse (2:20)
    b) Dire results (2:21)
    c) Disgusting behavior (2:22)

II. Christ will return (3:1–16)

  1. Denial of the parousia (3:1–4)
    a) Pastoral responsibility (3:1–2)
    b) Scoffers (3:3–4)

  2. The disproof (3:5–10)
    a) Cosmic convulsions (3:5–7)
    b) The delay of the parousia (3:8–10)

3. The last days and the moral life (3: 11–16)
   a) The change of the world and the conduct of men (3: 11–14)
   b) Making use of the time (3: 15–16)

The Close of the Letter (3: 17–18)

THE CLOSE OF THE LETTER (3: 17–18)

THE OPENING OF THE LETTER
(1:1-2)

THE ADDRESS (1: 1–2)

The epistle's salutation names its sender and recipient (1:1) and extends a blessing (1:2). In both verses the fundamental endowment of the Christian life is referred to: faith, knowledge. The work of salvation accomplished by our God and redeemer Jesus Christ begins with faith and comes to perfection in knowledge.

Faith

¹Simon Peter, a servant and apostle of Jesus Christ, to those who have obtained a faith of equal standing with ours in the righteousness of our God and saviour Jesus Christ.

Simon Peter is the apostle to whom Jesus entrusted the highest office; the church was to be built on him and the keys of the kingdom were given him. Both his names are given here: Simon, his personal name, and Peter (rock), the name given him by Jesus (Jn. 1:42). It is Peter, through the author of this epistle, who speaks to us.

Peter is "servant and apostle of Jesus Christ." He does not belong to himself, nor does he labor for himself. A servant is subordinate to his master; the apostle does not speak what he wishes, but what he has been commissioned to speak. Through his apostle, Jesus Christ is seen and heard. It is not the apostle's intention to inhibit access to the Lord, but rather to promote it.

Peter's apostleship is rooted in the faith. Faith is the teaching that came from Jesus; it is preached by the apostles and gives substance to the Christian life. Peter and his readers have the faith in common; it makes of the apostles and all believers one community. For all, it is equally precious. The Christian life is borne by the faith—to the very portals of the eternal kingdom. When the faith is threatened, it ceases to be taken for granted. Often its unique significance is only then recognized for the first time.

The Christian life does not result merely from human initiative, intelligence, and effort: it is based on the faith, and the faith is something only God can give. Because it is a gift, and a gratuitous one, the life that is built on it is also a gift and grace.

We owe our gift of faith to the righteousness of Jesus Christ. What does this mean? " Righteousness " includes all that Jesus did for our salvation. His atonement was " righteous " or " just," and abundantly so, inasmuch as he did the will of his heavenly Father perfectly, as the surrender of his life on the cross exemplifies. Proven by his " deed of righteousness," Jesus is raised to " God and saviour." He who was God and who condescended to the lowliness of human life becomes the saviour of all mankind. He uses his divine power now to bring salvation to those who have come to the faith. By the obedience of one man, we all are saved.

Knowledge (1 : 2)

[2]*May grace and peace be multiplied to you in the knowledge of God and of Jesus our Lord.*

Grace and peace sum up all the blessings of salvation showered upon the Christian. Grace is wished for us; it is the graciousness of God and the effect in us of this graciousness that make us pleasing in his eyes. And the gift of peace restores the order that man had disturbed by sin. The covenant that God contracted with Israel envisaged such a peace and now it is given in new glory by Christ, so that our lives may be inwardly put in order and that all men may live in a union formed by the love of God.

Both gifts are to be multiplied. On earth they are only a token and a beginning of the even greater blessings of salvation that await us. They will be multiplied in us according as our knowledge of Jesus Christ grows in us. Such knowledge is not mere information given at a moment's notice; it is an understanding fostered by the faith, a wholehearted assent to and penetration of all one's life by the avowal: Jesus is Lord. It is especially our experience of Jesus Christ that grows throughout a lifetime union with him. Jesus encounters us in his holy gospel, in the sacrament of the altar, in our neighbor—day after day. In all this we are to come to know and love him more and more deeply, until we live in him in faith and in peace.

THE BODY OF THE LETTER
(1:3—3:16)

ADHERENCE TO THE TEACHING HANDED DOWN (1:3-21)

The Second Epistle of Peter was written to counteract certain false prophets (2:1) who have not yet cut themselves off from the Christian community (2:13) but who lead a life that contradicts traditional teaching (3:3). Their motto is " freedom " (2:19) and, therefore, they do not bother themselves about moral codes; they give their instincts and passions free rein (2:10. 14. 18). The heathen vices that they foreswore in baptism, or should have foresworn, are beginning to appear in their conduct again (2:18f.). They are libertines who think that knowledge has made them perfect.

They have no respect for the " holy commandment " (2:21), the teaching handed down; they either reject it or interpret it as they wish. One essential datum of the faith is that of the second coming of Christ, the final judgment, and the salvation of the last days. This is the truth they deny. Their argument is based on experience: the Christian community has already waited many years for the second coming, in the belief that it was imminent—but it has not taken place. The false prophets " know " that these final events have already occurred and therefore are not to be awaited any more.

The epistle takes up a position against the false teaching on the non-existence of moral obligations (libertinism) and against the denial of the second coming and related phenomena. The epistle first warns that the teaching handed down must be adhered to (1:3-21); then it refutes the false theories (2:1—3:16).

Moral Effort (1:3-11)

The gifts of God received in baptism are the beginning of salvation, but they are not its full realization (1:3-4). They demand zeal for

133

moral goodness (1:5–7) if definitive salvation is to be attained (1:8–11).

The Way of Salvation (1:3–4)

³His divine power has granted to us all things that pertain to life and godliness, through the knowledge of him who called us to be his own glory and excellence . . .

The divine power of Jesus Christ has granted us all things that pertain to salvation: grace, faith, remission of sin, divine strength, union with God, the Holy Spirit. Christ activated and confirmed this gift in us at our baptism. What he gave us then he will not take back, unless we make it necessary. He has not done anything halfway, but has given us everything we need. " All things that pertain to our salvation " means everything that pertains to our life and godliness. The life we draw from Jesus finds expression in godliness, in honoring God, in relating one's life to him and doing his will. The life we presently lead carries within it a promise of the future: " Wait for the mercy of our Lord Jesus Christ unto eternal life " (Jude 21).

We attain to salvation by the knowledge of him who has called us. From our point of view, the beginning of the way of salvation is the faith—knowledge of Jesus Christ. Without this knowledge in faith no one can come to salvation. But from the point of view of God, who works through Jesus Christ, the first thing is that we are " called." Only if he calls us is the door to knowledge opened. And God provides the means to attain that to which he calls us.

Jesus calls us by his glory and excellence (of virtue). The divine glory and power are his by nature. And the " excellence of virtue " is his because he does in all things the will of God. " If one loves justice, the fruits of her works are virtues; for she teaches moderation and prudence, justice and fortitude, and nothing in life is more useful for men than these " (Wis. 8:7). Jesus calls us and gives us a participation in his glory and excellence of life.

What is called life and godliness in verse 3a is called glory and excellence in verse 3b. The salvation that Christ accomplishes in us is a many-sided phenomenon. In both descriptions given here, the first word sets the divine gift in the foreground: the life and glory of God. Who does not see that both of these are purely gifts? The second word in each pairing looks more to the human accomplishment: godliness and virtue. The two work together—the gift of God and human effort. But in the final analysis it is the living God who creates all in all.

4. . . . by which he has granted to us his precious and very great promises, that through these you may escape from the corruption that is in the world because of passion, and become partakers of the divine nature.

Everything that has been given us is given with a view to definitive salvation. Besides everything else we received in baptism and that characterizes our Christian life, we have also received precious and very great promises. What God has begun, he will bring to final perfection. The life that Christ gave us is itself a promise of something more precious and more magnificent that awaits us.

That something is: participation in the divine nature. God

wills to allow us to share in his divine glory! The New Testament writers experimented with a wealth of expressions and images in their attempt to express the ineffable something that awaits those who have won definitive salvation. The Second Epistle of Peter uses an expression that was familiar to Greek philosophy. It is perhaps less graphic than some others, but it gets to the essential point: participation in the divine essence, and therefore participation in the very life of God. This is beyond our powers of comprehension; our deepest desires for self-realization, for perfection, and happiness will be fulfilled. Who can understand what that entails?

The person who has not escaped from the corruption that is in the world because of passion will not realize this promise. The antithesis of future participation in the divine nature is perdition, just as eternal life is the antithesis of the death that is damnation. He who wants to share in the life of God must keep far from perdition. But how? Perdition is the lot of him who succumbs to his unruly desires. And they are aroused by " the world." As is often so in the New Testament, " world " here refers to the sphere of evil, of sin; the world that opposes God. John can say of this world: " All that is in the world, the lust of the flesh and the lust of the eyes and the pride of life, is not of the Father but is of the world " (1 Jn. 2:16). This " world " excites the sexual urge, the greed for possessions, and the pride of the self-satisfied man who wants to be independent of God. The man who is determined to follow his passions and never deny himself anything to which they attract him will transgress the will of God, will fall victim to sin, and thereby subject to corruption. " Friendship with the world is enmity with God " (Jas. 4:4). God has begun the work of our salvation, but its completion is not yet a fact. The tension between what is already possessed and what is not yet possessed demands a moral testing. The final state of salvation can be attained. God wills that we exert ourselves. Only then will we gain permanent possession of what we have so far. This tension also offers us encouragement. Jesus has already given us all that we need for success. Our " godliness " comes from the life he has given us; our " virtue " comes from the divine glory that he shares with us. Thus we are kept alert and led on by the holy hope that is the beacon of our life.

Development of the Moral Life (1 : 5–7)

Man must by his own life give answer to the divine initiative. According to one literary form, the several virtues compose a " chain "; one virtue has its root in another, just as one link of a chain is anchored in the link next to it. Faith and charity provide the framework of this chain of virtue. Besides these two, six more virtues are named. They can be paired: virtue and knowledge, self-control and patience, fear of God and love of neighbor. The first pair develops personal initiative, the second overcomes the obstacles to moral perfection, the third governs one's relationship to God and man. Thus is the Christian life ordered by faith and love, in peace with God, with other men, and with oneself.

5For this very reason make every effort to supplement your faith with virtue, and virtue with knowledge, 6and knowledge with self-control, and self-control with steadfastness, and steadfastness with godliness, 7and godliness with brotherly affection, and brotherly affection with love.

" Making every effort, supplement your faith." In other words, be willing to " pay the cost " to pursue virtue in the faith. In the city of ancient times, the citizens turned out for the great occasions of military, artistic, and athletic performances; each one had to make a personal contribution—and it was usually considerable. So too the Christian must be prepared to " pay something " for salvation. In his teaching Jesus made it very clear that entrance to the kingdom of God demands the utmost application of all one's powers.

Faith is put at the beginning of the chain of virtues, and love at its terminus. Faith is the source, and love the goal. Love is founded on faith; like a tree it grows from its roots. The tree of faith continually produces new branches, leaves, and buds, so that new fruits of charity can mature. In the end there is a faith penetrated and fructified by love alone. Or, in terms of a bridge, faith and love are the piles that support it over a stream. Faith and love ensure that the entire construct of the virtues will be truly Christian. Each virtue must have the true fundament and be ordered to the one true goal. The whole superstructure of the virtues is supported by the pillars of faith and love. Neither faith without love, nor love without faith, is pleasing to God.

" Supplement your faith with virtue." Faith is the source of the Christian life. All virtue is rooted in it. " Virtue " has become for us a word that makes one think of " bourgeois " morality or fatuous " goodness." But something vigorous is meant by the term; virtue in the New Testament is the hall-mark of the person who does in all things the will of God. Thus perfect faith is dedication to God's word and will. The man who thinks that the entire function of faith is the assent of reason to revealed truths will hardly understand this. But he who understands faith in its biblical sense, namely that it involves both assent to truth and dedication to the God of revelation, will understand it correctly.

"Supplement virtue with knowledge." We saw already that knowledge is not only a matter of intellectual comprehension, but a loving self-involvement. Effort to lead a morally good life creates a sensitivity to the things of God and to our responsibilities. "It is my prayer that your love may abound more and more, with knowledge and all (moral) discernment" (Phil. 1:9). Morally good conduct is always accompanied by increased knowledge. In the light given us by God, we see things around us differently—our work, our fellow men. This light will help us to understand our everyday world better.

"And knowledge with self-control." Whoever wants to progress in the way of knowledge must learn self-control. He knows the values that are of primary concern to him—and he knows how many unimportant things there are on which we squander our time. The self-controlled man knows especially how to tame his passions and desires; he is their master. This is not weakness but power brought under control; our passions and desires easily effervesce. Self-control is mentioned in connection with justice (Acts 24:25); it is essential in the effort to please God. All who would attain salvation must practice it.

"And self-control with steadfastness." Self-control leads to steadfastness; the self-controlled person knows that the highest goods can be won only by courageous and persevering struggle. Steadfastness is a sustaining power that strengthens and encourages. The person who can control his passions can also persevere in the difficulties and hardships that come from without. The person who tries to satisfy all his natural inclinations will never be able to muster up perseverance in afflictions. Self-control and steadfastness are related to faith and love. For the perfection of faith in love—for the transition from the beginning of salvation to its consummation—self-control and steadfastness are necessary: we are always and on all sides threatened. " You have need of endurance, so that you may do the will of God and receive what is promised " (Heb. 10:36). " Let us run with perseverance the race that is set before us " (Heb. 12:1).

" And steadfastness with godliness." Only he who perseveres in the struggle against unruly passions and against the powers opposed to God truly worships God. It is no longer mere lip-service, empty talk, but proven, purified godliness. It has assimilated the whole of life to itself: all one's experiences and trials, joys and sufferings, have grown like a tree from the light of the sun and the rain of storms.

" And godliness with brotherly affection." True godliness will always manifest itself in an active love: it is its measure and goal. The exchange of love in the Christian community is especially thought of here; sympathetic concern for others, the unostentatious helping hand, the care of brothers and sisters in need. " Religion that is pure and undefiled before God and the Father is this: to visit orphans and widows in their affliction " (Jas. 1:27). " If anyone says, ' I love God,' and hates his brother, he is a liar " (1 Jn. 4:20). To see and love God in other men is an expression of godliness, for God has created man in his own image. What we have done or not done to the least of our brothers, we have done or not done to Jesus.

" And brotherly affection with love." The love of our neighbor in the spirit of Christ results from that supernatural love (agape) that God communicates to us; it is a reflection of God's own love. Christian fraternal charity is not a mere humanitarianism, but the expression of a love that gives of itself, an expression of living for others. It is a reflection of what John says: " God is love " (1 Jn. 4:16). Agape is the crowning glory of the ensemble of the virtues, the final link in the chain of virtues. He who loves fulfills the law and the prophets. Love sums up the whole Christian life in itself. It is the "bond of perfection" (Col. 3:14). In all that we think and do we should strive for this love.

Virtue and Perfection (*1:8–11*)

The cultivation of virtue leads to the knowledge of Christ (1:8–9) and prepares the way into the kingdom of Christ (1:10–11). The Christian is ordered to this goal and must live with it always in mind.

KNOWLEDGE OF CHRIST (1:8–9)

[8]For if these things are yours and abound, they keep you from being ineffective or unfruitful in the knowledge of our Lord Jesus Christ. [9]For whoever lacks these things is blind and short-sighted and has forgotten that he was cleansed from his old sins.

The goal of the Christian life is the knowledge of our Lord Jesus Christ—perfect knowledge and lasting union with him. "And this is eternal life, that they know thee the only true God, and Jesus Christ whom thou hast sent" (Jn. 17:13). This goal will only be reached if our life is rich in good works. The harvest and fruit of life is the knowledge of Christ, in fact participation in his divine glory. Everything that God has sown in us by giving us opportunities for good works is to come to fruition. God has sown the seed in our hearts, but we must do our part so as to bring forth fruit. And yet it remains true that growth and fruition is not something entirely within our control.

The person who takes no interest in a virtuous life is blind and shortsighted, for he does not see what Jesus Christ expects of his life. He is deprived of the use of his eyes and of the healthy vision that perceives the true goal of life. He has forgotten that in baptism he was cleansed of the sins he had committed in his former life. The remembrance of this cleansing should have made it clear to him that a sinless life was expected of him.

The Christian life begins with baptism and leads to the consummation of salvation. We build on the fundament that God has laid. God wills that the structure be completed, but not without our coöperation. In the sacraments God does what the sacrament signifies; the cleansing bath of baptism accomplishes a cleansing from sin. But the one who receives the sacrament must remind himself of this purification. We must often look at ourselves to see what we really are and what is in fact the fundament, the principle, of our life.

Entry into the Kingdom of Christ (1:10–11)

¹⁰*Therefore, brethren, be the more zealous to confirm your call and election, for if you do this you will never fall.*

God's call and election are the beginning of salvation. Both precede baptism. Without being called or chosen, a person cannot enter the eternal kingdom. But God's call and election have to be confirmed, rendered valid and definitive. This depends on our interest and effort. God has initiated the work of salvation, he has extended his beneficent love to us—without our doing anything; but he wills to give us eternal salvation only with our coöperation.

The person who exerts himself will not forfeit salvation. But the possibility of eternal damnation is not excluded for the one called and chosen to grace. The requirements for acceptance into the kingdom of God must be met. Jesus names such requirements in the eight beatitudes. The Second Epistle of Peter also names the virtues required for entrance into the kingdom of Christ. The eternal beatitude to which we are called will be ours only if we do the will of God.

¹¹*So there will be richly provided for you an entrance into the eternal kingdom of our Lord and saviour Jesus Christ.*

If we exert ourselves, God will admit us to the eternal kingdom. He demands of us deeds. Final salvation is also a gift of God, but one that he gives only on the basis of works that have been pleasing to him. God gives salvation in abundance; what he gives far exceeds what man could achieve by himself alone.

God admits us to the eternal kingdom of our Lord and saviour Jesus Christ. Jesus proclaims the kingdom and glory of God; the Second Epistle of Peter proclaims the kingdom and glory of Christ. God has given dominion to the Son and he wills to give us his divine kingdom through Christ, if we will recognize him as our Lord and put our hope in his deed of salvation. The full knowledge of Christ and the kingdom of Christ are the same glorious salvation that God wills to give us through his Son. The first expression emphasizes the happiness of the individual, the second the salvation of the community. Jesus Christ, our Lord and redeemer, is the fullness of that which we await. In him God wills to open to us the fullness of his riches.

At the end of this section we know why the faith is precious (1:1): everything that it brings is precious—participation in the divine nature, calling and election, fruition, the knowledge of

Christ and the kingdom of Christ, glory and power. Truly, everything that is " necessary for life " (1 : 3). But if we do not accept the faith and live according to its laws, then blindness and shortsightedness—in short, perdition—will be our lot.

Belief in the Second Coming of Christ (1:12–21)

The false prophets who deny that the baptized are under moral restrictions are also unwilling to accept the traditional teaching that Jesus will come a second time. After stating its credentials (1 : 12–15), the epistle proclaims the certainty of the second coming: it is guaranteed by the word of God at the transfiguration of Christ (1 : 16–18) and by the Old Testament prophecies that undoubtedly will be fulfilled (1 : 19–21).

Pastoral Concern (1 :12–15)

The author of the Second Epistle of Peter was totally dedicated to the salvation of men. As someone charged with a pastoral office, he feels responsible for the spiritual welfare of the faithful (1 : 12), and so much the more as he knows he has not long to live (1 : 13f.); the letter he is writing will be his last will and testament (1 : 15).

PASTORAL REMINDER (1 : 12)

12Therefore, I intend always to remind you of these things, though you know them and are established in the truth that you have.

Pastoral concern takes the form of reminding the faithful, of recalling the truth to them. The pastoral ministry of the prophets had taken a similar form: " Remember this and consider, recall it to mind, you transgressors, remember the former things of old; for I am God, and there is no other; I am God and there is none like me " (Is. 46:8). The Book of Deuteronomy contains many instances of such thinking and reminding. A monitum to fidelity to the law is supported by the reminder of God's salvific deeds for his people: " You shall remember that you were a servant in the land of Egypt, and the Lord your God brought you thence with a mighty hand and an outstretched arm; therefore, the Lord your God commanded you to keep the sabbath day " (Deut. 5:15).

The New Testament proclamation is a reminder of the word and work of Jesus. The Holy Spirit brings to mind all that Jesus had said (Jn. 14:26). He keeps and explains the word and work of Jesus; he keeps them alive in the world and convinces men of their truth. The church's liturgy also has a commemorative function. Its center is the eucharistic celebration, which is at once a commemoration and a reminder. The celebration of Passover, of which the Eucharist is the fulfillment, also had a commemorative function. " He has caused his wonderful works to be remembered " (Ps. 111:4). We celebrate in action the remembrance of the death of the Lord when we eat the eucharistic bread and drink from the chalice (1 Cor. 11:26).

The pastor admits that the faithful know what he is saying to them, but he also realizes that they need to have the truth repeated anew. The truth is the gospel, in which the power of God dwells. Thus remembrance does not mean simply to recall to mind something that happened in the past. Rather, the power that is latent in the sacred words is brought to the surface and ushered into the church of the present. The preaching of the truth is the advent, the " parousia," of the truth. It is not by chance that the same word is used for the coming of the truth and for the mighty coming of the Lord in the final aeon. When a priest, as counselor or confessor, reminds us of a point of faith, his advice comes from his concern for our salvation. We forget all too easily and need to be aroused and shaken, even if the one who warns us seems a nuisance. Parents must remind their children, and every Christian his dormant brother.

An Imperious Duty (1:13–14)

¹³*I think it right, as long as I am in this body [tent], to arouse you by way of reminder, *¹⁴*since I know that the putting off of my body will be soon, as our Lord Jesus Christ showed me.*

God has commissioned his minister to keep the faithful alert by reminding them. Preparedness is the state of mind that Jesus had insisted on in his discourses on the last things. A state of preparedness will be kept alive by frequently meditating on the last things, especially the second coming of Christ. We will not rightly see all that confronts us in life if we do not view it with reference to the last things.

Only a short time remains for the accomplishment of our work. Our life is like that of a nomad who has no fixed abode. Hardly has he pitched his tent when he must take it down again. Our life is passed in the earthly tent of the human body; death is the folding of that tent. " The soul dwells in a mortal tent." We must do what we can as long as we still have the opportunity. Jesus said: " We must work the works of him who sent me, while it is day; night comes, when no one can work "

(Jn. 9:4). For the Christian, " the last things " in his life should not petrify him but urge him on to activity. The long wait for the coming of Christ has focussed our attention too exclusively on the fate of the individual—death, trial, eternal happiness or damnation. When we think of " the last things," this is usually what we think of. But we are all also kept for the final occurrences that will affect all mankind and the whole world.

Peter knows that he will soon die. Jesus has told him that he would undergo martyrdom in his old age (Jn. 21:18f.). The author of the epistle probably knew too of a tradition that Peter had received a revelation of the exact date of his death. Again, the message for us is clear: even the knowledge of the proximity of death should not stupefy us but urge us to expend all our energy in doing what is right before God.

BEYOND THE GRAVE (1:15)

[15]*And I will see to it that after my departure you may be able at any time to recall these things.*

The beginning of salvation—our calling and election—are not gifts in which we can rest. They demand effort until the final goal is attained. The minister of the gospel is not satisfied simply to have preached the message of salvation. Even when faith, conversion, and baptism follow his preaching, he is still bound to continual effort to see to it that remembrance of the great deeds of salvation remains in clear focus. The depiction of the conscientious minister is awesome: his efforts reach from beyond the grave. Must not his zeal be a stimulus to the persons for whom he takes such pains?

How will Peter keep alive the recollection of these things? What does he intend to leave behind so that the faithful will be kept reminded of these things after his death? We think first of all of the epistle we are reading; it is a kind of testament to his care for the faithful. One's last will is a document that bespeaks urgency, seriousness, and responsibility. Who is going to merely " chat " at his last hour? A written document will make the voice of the Apostle discernible even after his death. The spoken word is ephemeral; the written word perdures and safeguards. The Apostle wants his word always to be present.

The Transfiguration and Parousia of Christ (1:16–18)

The faithful know of the teaching on the second coming of Christ, but they should not be annoyed to be reminded of it once again. Pastoral solicitude knows no limits. The second coming of Christ in glory is not a truth that was spun out by human cleverness; it is founded on the revelation of Christ's glory at the transfiguration (1:16). The word of God had identified Jesus as the Messiah and bringer of salvation. He will come in glory and power, to establish the eternal kingdom (1:17f.).

THE SURE FUNDAMENT (1:16)

¹⁶*For we did not follow cleverly devised myths when we made known to you the power and coming of our Lord Jesus Christ, but we were eyewitnesses of his majesty.*

" We have made known to you the power and coming of our Lord." This coming of Christ in majesty is an essential component of the Christian proclamation. His coming will be in great power and glory (Mk. 13:27). According to the eschatological proclamation, he will be surrounded by angels and will appear on the clouds of heaven (Mk. 13:26). He will be victorious over all powers that oppose him (2 Thess. 2:8). The world will be shaken by his mighty presence (Mk. 13:25f.). In preaching this the apostles are not following cleverly devised myths. Those who deny the second coming of Christ call the proclamations of the second coming " sophistic "—consciously deceptive invention. They call them pernicious myths, fairy tales. They differ, therefore, from those who today deny the second coming, though the moderns also use the word " myth." The false prophets mentioned in the epistle accuse the apostles of conscious deception; the modern sceptics hold that this teaching was the product of human desires to which nothing in reality corresponds.

The apostles are not spinners of fairy tales. They speak as eyewitnesses of the power and glory of Christ. To be sure, none of the apostles could actually see the second coming of Christ, but God had given them a quick glimpse of the future event: the appearance of Christ in power and glory. The apostles—Peter includes himself with the others—had been eyewitnesses of Christ's glory in the transfiguration. The gospels name three apostles as these witnesses: Peter, John, and James (Mt. 17: 1-8). The important thing is that these three were eyewitnesses; they have not invented a story, but simply reported what they themselves had seen. Their statements about Christ are based on historical fact.

THE DIVINE REVELATION (1:17-18)

17For when he received honor and glory from God the Father

and the voice was borne to him by the Majestic Glory, " This is
my beloved Son, with whom I am well pleased," . . .

The glory of God irradiated Jesus. The visible sign of it was the
light present. " His garments became glistening, intensely white,
as no fuller on earth could bleach them " (Mk. 9:3). " His face
shone like the sun, and his garments became white as light "
(Mt. 17:2). The honor that Jesus received was divine honor.

The voice that spoke about Jesus came from the exalted glory
that is God. God's word about the transfigured Jesus explains
his glory and might: he is Son of God, the beloved, the Son
with whom God is well pleased. God is named Father; it explains and founds Jesus' titles: God and saviour (1:1), God and
Lord (1:2). We now understand correctly: the glory of God is
also the glory of Jesus. The power with which Christ will appear
in his second coming is included in it. God has so endowed and
glorified him. Only by the word of the Father could the disciples
understand the mysterious event on Mount Tabor. There is much
that only God's word can make understandable to us: the
meaning of history and of one's own life. God's revelatory word
lays bare to us what was intended and what its true import is.

[18] . . . *we heard this voice borne from heaven, for we were with*
him on the holy mountain.

The apostles heard what they later reported. They heard the voice
of God. The mountain is called a holy mountain: it was the
place where the glorious revelation was given. The apostles both
saw and heard their Lord. " Blessed are your eyes, for they see,
and your ears, for they hear " (Mt. 13:16). The double witness-
ing gives our faith a doubly certain basis. We, it is true, did not

ourselves see and hear these events. But in what God lets us see and hear, we can ourselves experience his presence and power. In the words of the gospel preached in the church we hear his mighty word. In the performance of every liturgical celebration, in the community that is the church, on the face of every fellow human, we see something of his glory. One must only know how to look.

The transfiguration was a foreglimpse of the glorious coming of Christ, of the parousia. Its historicity is a guarantee of the second coming of Christ in might. The one glorification of Christ is an earnest of the other. God's love of his Son will give him the final glorification which we await.

Old Testament Prophecy and the Parousia (1:19-21)

Two proofs of the second coming of Christ are given here: the transfiguration as an archetype of the salvation event and the word of prophecy (1:19). God speaks by his own word and by the facts of history. He who was an eyewitness of the transfiguration of Jesus, as were the apostles, has a surer grasp of prophecy than do the false prophets. The tradition based on apostolic eyewitnesses has a sounder claim to reliability than does the opinion of a heresiarch who was not an eyewitness. The writings of the Old Testament can be fully understood only in the light of the redemption wrought by Jesus Christ. The prophetic word requires, that is, an authoritative interpretation if it is not to lead into error (1:20f.).

THE WITNESS OF THE PROPHETIC WORD (1:19)

19And we have the prophetic word made more sure. You will do well to pay attention to this as to a lamp shining in a dark place, until the day dawns and the morning star rises in your hearts.

The prophetic word, preserved in the scriptures, speaks often of " the day of the Lord," when the Lord will come to holy judgment. All the prophets spoke of the day of the eschatological restoration of all things (Acts 3:20f.). They leave no doubt about the coming of the Lord in power. In the final analysis, all revelation in the Bible points to the plenary revelation of God's glory in the last times.

Sacred scripture is like a lamp shining in a darkened chamber. Such is the world in which we live. In order that we may find our way and not stray from the path willed by God, the word of God in the Bible gives us light.

We will need the light of God's prophetic word until the day dawns and the morning star rises in our hearts. Dawn (Rom. 13:12) and the rising of the morning star are the coming of Christ. When the Lord comes, the glory of Christ will radiate on us; we will be illuminated and transfigured by his effulgent glory. All darkness will then be dissipated; there will be no more going astray, no falling aside. When the light that is dimly evident in the scriptures shines in full brilliance, it will not require sacred writings any longer. But until then?

CORRECT INTERPRETATION OF THE PROPHETIC WORD (1:20–21)

20First of all, you must understand this, that no prophecy of scripture is a matter of one's own interpretation, . . .

The false prophets also base themselves on the prophetic word of holy scripture (3:16). But the first rule for understanding the scriptures correctly is that scriptural prophecy cannot be interpreted according to one's personal whims. A prophecy is always something mysterious. The scriptures, and the prophecies they contain, include passages that need clarification. This is most apparent when we read the Old Testament and try to understand it by ourselves. How difficult that can be! How thankful we are when we find some help, some explanation, to show us the way. And yet how often we cannot understand, or completely misunderstand. The ability to understand scripture is a special gift of God.

21 . . . *because no prophecy ever came by the impulse of man, but men moved by the Holy Spirit spoke from God.*

Who can give a correct interpretation of the meaning of scripture? The first law for finding the meaning of scripture is: prophecy is not to be interpreted simply as it seems to the reader. This is how the false prophets interpret the scripture (3:16), and they distort its meaning. Prophecy does not originate in the human will; it is the work of the Holy Spirit. The men who spoke prophecies were borne by the Holy Spirit. He it was who inspired them to speak and to write. "The scriptures are inspired by God."

The prophets spoke from God. The liar-prophets " speak visions of their own minds, not from the mouth of the Lord " (Jer. 23:16). The true prophets did not speak from their own imaginings, but from God. They were holy because they were taken by God into his service and he spoke through them. The implications for the interpretation of prophecy are not explicitly drawn here. What would they be? Because holy scripture is not the invention and work of the human mind, its interpretation and explanation are not to be expected from men alone, but from God and the men whom he has taken into his service and qualified for their work. The interpretation of scripture must correspond to its inspiration.

Who are these men who can interpret scripture correctly? Certainly not everyone who reads the Bible, but only he whom God has empowered and enlightened *by the Holy Spirit*. But the Holy Spirit can come to someone who has no " office " in the church and give him a correct interpretation. This has happened countless times in the history of the church. But we cannot be sure of such an interpretation unless such " enlightened " men stand in harmony with tradition and submit themselves obediently to church authorities. The author of the epistle thinks especially of officials in the church whom God has appointed and to whom the grace of interpretation has been given with their grace of office. Thus the scriptures serve " the man of God " for his pastoral ministry in the church (2 Tim. 3:17). The " man of God " is a leader in the church. The true leaders are themselves led by God, so that they explain the true meaning of scripture. Thus can we have the certitude we seek in the whirlwind of opinions and interpretations.

RESISTING NEW DOCTRINE (2:1—3:16)

The faithful to whom the Second Epistle of Peter is addressed are threatened by false prophets. Their new teaching proclaims freedom from all moral law; the faithful dare not fall victim to this "libertinism" (2:1–22). The new "evangelists" also deny the second coming of the Lord; the faithful are not to let themselves be confused by their arguments (3:1–16).

False Teaching on Freedom (2:1–22)

What the false prophets are doing (2:1–3) will not go unpunished (2:4–9). The heresiarchs are exposed (2:10–14a) and their punishment stated (2:14b–19). What these men are about is a relapse into heathenism (2:20–22).

Liar-Prophets (2:1–3)

The teachers of truth sent by God are accompanied by liar-prophets, false messiahs, and false teachers. The church should not be surprised by this "law" of the history of revelation. The false prophets attack the Lord (2:1) and his people (2:2–3); they court damnation.

AGAINST THE LORD (2:1)

¹But false prophets also arose among the people, just as there will be false teachers among you, who will secretly bring in destruc-

155

tive heresies, even denying the master who bought them, bringing
upon themselves swift destruction.

Besides the true prophets there have always been false prophets
among the people of Israel who wooed the Israelites to idols and
pagan vices, promised them peace and earthly salvation, mocked
the oracles and threats of the true prophets. The New Testament
people of God are facing the same problem now. Teachers of
heresy are mingling with the teachers of truth. The New Testament people of God resembles the Old. The destinies of the Old
Testament people of God throw light on those of the New and
help us to understand our own situation better.

The false prophets arose from among the people. They give
themselves the appearance of piety and they fawn upon human
desires, but they have no mission from God. God permits false
prophets in his church, to test his people on their undivided love
of him and their ability to distinguish between truth and error.

The teaching spread by the false prophets leads to divisions
within the church; it destroys the unity of the church. He who
falsifies the teaching handed down in the church and broadcasts
doctrines that lead to perdition denies Christ as master and pos-
sessor, as he who alone has right of possession over the faithful.
He denies Christ the right that he has " bought " and gained at a
high price. We are Christ's own people and he watches over us
as our master. Whoever attacks his people, attacks Christ and his
rights. The teaching handed down is a sacrosanct treasure. The
Spirit of truth that Jesus has given his church and who leads it
to the full truth glorifies Christ, for " he will take what is mine
and declare it to you " (Jn. 16:13).

The false prophets bring upon themselves swift destruction.
Their fate is that of the false prophets of the Old Testament, of

whom it was said: " My hand will be against the prophets who
see delusive visions and who give lying divinations; . . . and you
shall know that I am the Lord God " (Ezek. 13:9). He who
tampers with the teaching of Christ condemns himself; his deed
is his condemnation. The truth is a great treasure given to the
church to be kept intact. In this matter there can be no com-
promise. To be sure, love is not to be betrayed and fidelity is not
to be confused with impatience. But we have no authority over
the truth revealed by God; it has authority over us.

AGAINST THE PEOPLE OF GOD (2:2–3)

*²And many will follow their licentiousness, and because of them
the way of truth will be reviled. ³And in their greed they will
exploit you with false words; from of old their condemnation has
not been idle, and their destruction has not been asleep.*

The false prophets are guilty of licentiousness. Their motto is
similar to that of the Corinthian libertines: " All things are law-
ful for me " (1 Cor. 6:12). Many follow their example. Man is
not particularly keen to resist the sexual urge, and anyone who
preaches that it is not wrong to enjoy oneself will find a ready
audience.

The false prophets still belong to the church. Thus their
immoral conduct imperils the whole church. Because of the false
prophets, the church is reviled by unbelievers. The teaching of
Jesus insists on a moral life flowing from unchangeable, divine
revelation. Just as the moral life of Christians should be an attrac-
tion to the way of truth, so their immoral conduct will be ground
for revilement of the holiness to which God has bound them.

The immoral conduct of Christians reflects on the truth of revelation, on Christ, and on God.

The false prophets are like devious businessmen. Their high-sounding propaganda is nothing but deceit. They speak of moral freedom, of the power of the spirit, of the knowledge they possess and teach to others; but behind it all there lurks the destruction that they let loose upon men. Their zeal is greed; they are not teachers and apostles who speak by divine commission, but unscrupulous tradesmen after money (2:14). Their attitude is the antithesis of Christ's, who gave his life a ransom for many (Mk. 10:45).

"From of old their condemnation has not been idle." They occasion serious problems for believers. How explain the success of the false prophets? How explain their popularity? Why does God not intervene? Why does the divine judge not act? Why does he restrain his hand? God is not asleep, he is not inactive. The judgment has long been underway. It is as much present in history as is his mercy.

Just Judgment (2:4-9)

Three instances of punishment from the Book of Genesis show that the ungodly do not go unpunished and that God spares the just. The false prophets think that they counter the warning of punishment and damnation by their hope: "God will spare us; in all his punishments, never have all perished; some always escape death." The Second Epistle of Peter intends to disprove this. Only a few are spared—the just. Historical instances of divine retribution are not yet the final judgment. The unjust who escape punishment in the course of human history are not exempted from the last judgment. The three instances of punishment cited here are those of God vis-à-vis the angels (2:4), the generation of the deluge (2:5), and the inhabitants of Sodom and Gomorrah (2:6–8).

THE PUNISHMENT OF THE ANGELS (2:4)

⁴For if God did not spare the angels when they sinned, but cast them into hell and committed them to pits of nether gloom to be kept until the judgment; . . .

Angels have sinned. No information is given here as to what the angels did. But in the Epistle of Jude we read: " The angels that did not keep their own position but left their proper dwelling . . . acted immorally and indulged in unnatural lust " (Jude 6f.). This relates to Genesis 6:2: " The sons of God saw that the daughters of men were fair; and they took to wife such of them as they chose." But Peter gives no indication of how the angels had sinned; he simply states the fact. The scriptures contain mysteries to which we cannot give a satisfactory solution.

The angels are privileged creatures of God, and yet they were not spared when they sinned. In judgment God does not look to the person but the deed (Rom. 2:6. 11). The false prophets have an exalted notion of God's gifts—so exalted that they assume they can sin and nevertheless not fall victim to divine punishment. The Epistle to the Romans speaks in a similar way of the false prophets who said: " Let us continue in sin, so that grace may be increased " (Rom. 6:1). The gifts of salvation that we already possess do not exempt us from the duty of shunning immorality and of fearing God's judgment. An abundance of grace should inspire us to humility and not to presumption.

God has committed the fallen angels to pits of nether gloom. " Tartarus " was one of the names used at that time for the place of eternal punishment. It was thought of as a dark subterranean cave. The fallen angels were banned from the radiant face of God to the torment of separation from him, that is, to darkness. But they have not yet endured their definitive punishment. They are being kept for the more severe and definitive punishment that will be inflicted on them when Christ comes. The second coming of Christ brings with it the final judgment.

THE PUNISHMENT BY FLOOD (2:5)

[5] *. . . if he did not spare the ancient world, but preserved Noah, a herald of righteousness, with seven other persons, when he brought a flood upon the world of the ungodly; . . .*

God did not spare the ancient world. The Second Epistle of Peter knows three worlds: the ancient world before the deluge, the present world and the world of the future (3:13). The ancient world was God's creation also and he loved it, for " he saw that it was very good " (Gen. 1:31). He loved the men of this world, for they were his image (Gen. 1:27). And yet he did not spare this world and its inhabitants when they renounced him.

Only Noah and his family—his wife, his three sons, and their wives—were spared. God saved Noah—and the others for his sake—because Noah was a " herald of righteousness." He preached conversion and penance (1 Pet. 3:20). Because he was righteous, he had no fear of divine punishment. Divine punishment is not an indiscriminate sentence of perdition. He who does God's will, remains faithful in God's service, will not be swept along in a universal sentence of punishment; he will be protected by God.

The deluge is attributed directly to God. It comes upon the world because of evil men. World and man compose a unit. The world was created for man; it is also included in the guilt and punishment of man. The punishment of the deluge came over the world because it had distanced itself from its source and had rejected the holy will of God.

THE PUNISHMENT OF SODOM AND GOMORRAH (2:6–8)

6 . . . if by turning the cities of Sodom and Gomorrah to ashes he condemned them to extinction and made them an example to those who were to be ungodly; 7 and if he rescued righteous Lot, greatly distressed by the licentiousness of the wicked, 8 (for by what that righteous man saw and heard as he lived among them, he was vexed in his righteous soul day after day with their lawless deeds), . . .

The destruction of Sodom and Gomorrah by fire (Gen. 19) was at once a divine punishment and a warning for future ages. The scriptures were written for our instruction. Only Lot was exempted from the destruction, for he was just and was not guilty of the incontinence that was rampant all around him. His was a martyrdom, to persevere in doing the will of God amid universal unconcern. It was heroism to live a pure life among the impure.

The righteous man who lives among the unrighteous is vexed in his soul. Pictures, images, words, and deeds surround him, harass him, try to entice him to incontinence. The parenthesis that elaborates on this facet of his experience suggests the image of a prison: at the beginning his seeing and hearing are mentioned, and at the end the lawless deeds he must witness. The righteous man lives in such an atmosphere, day after day. The people round him are victims of their own bodies; their life is debauchery. God is aware of such sufferings, such martyrdom, and heroism; in the hour of judgment on sinners, the man who has remained strong in temptation will also receive his due.

Twofold Outcome (2: 9–10a)

[9] *. . . then the Lord knows how to rescue the godly from trial, and to keep the unrighteous under punishment until the day of judgment,* [10a]*and especially those who indulge in the lust of defiling passion and despise authority.*

From the three punishments recorded in the Old Testament the consequences are now drawn. First, the Lord knows. That is the answer to the question: Why does the Lord not intervene, as he has in the great punishments of earlier times? Jesus is Lord of the just and the unjust. He sees and hears and knows each and every person and will not relinquish his sovereignty.

The Lord rescues the godly from their trials. Conflict and misery are to test them, but their trials will strengthen them in patience (Jas. 1:2). Even if the just man suffers as much as did Job, he knows that the Lord will rescue him. God permitted the trials of Noah, " herald of justice " though he was; he ordained that Lot obey the divine will in a decadent environment. It is not numbers and " the crowd " that are decisive in God's sight, but purity of life, even that of a single individual.

The unjust, who do not do the will of God, are kept for the day of judgment. Even if God does not punish them straightaway, it does not mean that they have eluded just retribution. The day of judgment looms over every human act.

Incontinence cannot be indulged in with impunity. The three punishments were inflicted, according to the biblical passages, because of incontinence. The fall of the angels is related to lack of self-control in sexual matters. The introduction to the story of the deluge alludes to the decline in marital morals (Gen. 6: 1ff.); the destruction of the two cities of sin was due to unnatural sexual aberrations. The incontinent cater to their passions and to the defilement of the body. Incontinence is like a mistress whom the incontinent follow, a teacher whose disciples trail after him. Instead of following the Lord, lust creates for itself a following. " Their god is the belly " (Phil. 3: 19). By their conduct they also contemn the lordship of Christ, their Lord (Jude 8). He has purchased them and therefore they belong to him, body and soul; but the incontinent abuse the Lord's possession.

Rooting out the False Prophets (2 : 10b–14)

The shamelessness of the false prophets registers in their conduct (2:10b–12) and pleasure-seeking (2:13–14a). Verse 10a has already indicated the division of this section.

REVILERS (2:10b–12)

The false prophets have no respect for anything (2:10b–11). The key word of the passage is " revile." It occurs three times. The false prophets are shameless, insolent, and presumptuous. Therefore, their end will be disgraceful (2:12).

[10b]*Bold and willful, they are not afraid to revile the glorious ones, [11]whereas angels, though greater in might and power, do not pronounce a reviling judgment upon them before the Lord.*

The Christian submits himself in reverence to the dominion of Christ, whereas the false prophets deny that Christ is the Lord. The man of reverence regards "the glorious ones," the evil spirits, with awe, but the false prophets think themselves mightier than Satan, mightier than the evil spirits. The reverential man respects the laws and decisions of God, but the false prophets pay no attention to God's moral laws. Even if we are sure of God's love and paternal care, this certainly does not lessen a filial fear of him.

The angels, who excel man in "power and might," have respect for one another; they did not speak a word of condemnation over the fallen angels (Jude 9). How much more must the man who has been ransomed by Jesus Christ have a holy fear of the angelic powers and not think himself superior to them. What is reprobated here is not a disavowal of satanic powers opposed to God, not hatred of evil, but the self-assured presumption characteristic of these strange "Christians." They have the idea that they can judge all things from their elevated point of view and that they are not threatened by any danger. God has called us to humility; of our own knowledge and ability, we have "nothing to boast of."

Incontinence and irreverence are closely linked in the false prophets. Paul refutes the proponents of sexual libertinism with the reminder of the fullness of grace that also penetrates the body of the Christian: "Do you not know that your body is a temple of the Holy Spirit within you, which you have from God? You are not your own; you were bought with a price. So glorify God in your body" (1 Cor. 6:19f.).

[12]*But these, like irrational animals, creatures of instinct, born to be caught and killed, reviling in matters of which they are*

ignorant, will be destroyed in the same destruction with them,
[13a]*suffering wrong for their wrongdoing.*

What happens to these shameless men, who are " like irrational animals," is what happens to animals: capture and death. The incontinent bring destruction with them and will themselves be destroyed. They do what is wrong and they will reap the reward of their wrongdoing. God will treat them without respect, even as they have treated him and his creation.

REVELERS (2:13–14)

The false prophets pander to the vices that are often mentioned in the lists of vices in the New Testament: voluptuousness (2:13b), incontinence (2:14a), and greed (2:14b).

[13b]*They count it pleasure to revel in the daytime. They are blots and blemishes, reveling in their dissipation, carousing with you.*

The avocation of these new apostles of moral licentiousness is revelry. They did not take their meals in the evening, as was the custom, but during the daytime. Eating and drinking are what they live for. Even the love-feast associated with the celebration of the Eucharist serves them as an opportunity to indulge in their favorite pleasures. Their lack of respect does not even shrink from the All Holy. In view of such abuses, the agitation and harsh judgment of the epistle become more understandable.

[14a]*They have eyes full of adultery, insatiable for sin.*

Where revelry is going on, incontinence is never far away. Even the celebration of the Agape is for these men an opportunity to pamper their adulterous inclinations by looks and desires. The holy celebration serves to satisfy the lust of these " blots and blemishes."

[14b]*They entice unsteady souls. They have hearts trained in greed. Accursed children!*

Their zealous " apostolate " is directed to recent converts and to those Christians who are not yet well grounded in faith and morals. But this zeal originates in greed. Their " apostolic " activity is not for the glorification of God and the salvation of souls; it springs from avarice (2:3). Avarice poisons the apostolate.

When these vices are disguised under a religious mask they are so much the more hateful and reprehensible. Even the sanctuary can be invaded by man's sinfulness. But revelry, incontinence, and greed will be cursed by God. They who give themselves to these sins are accursed children—already under a divine curse. The abuses in the community and the conduct of its delinquent members will be brought to light. Nothing will remain hidden. We know that the more grace one is given, the greater is the duty to live according to it. Disorder and debauchery in the life of a Christian—especially when they are in some way connected with the holy service before God—are more grievous in God's sight than the same actions when done by those who do not know God's will.

Fruitless Frenzy (2:15–19)

The false prophets are very energetic in their efforts; they are the quintessence of busyness. What value does their activity have in God's sight? Holy scripture (2:15–16) and nature (2:17–19) show that their activity is vacuous. Scripture and nature are sources of divine wisdom, for both are the word of God—in writing and in work.

VEERING FROM THE RIGHT WAY (2:15–16)

¹⁵Forsaking the right way they have gone astray; they have followed the way of Balaam, the son of Beor, who loved gain from wrongdoing, ¹⁶but was rebuked for his own transgression; a dumb ass spoke with human voice and restrained the prophet's madness.

The judgment on the false prophets is: they have forsaken the right way and have gone astray—because of their revelry, incontinence, and greed. The right way, the way of God, is the truth handed down. What the false prophets proclaim is in fact a false way, the path followed by unrestrained passions.

The way of the false prophets is compared with the way of Balaam (Num. 22–24). He was supposed to put a curse on the people of Israel but God forbad him. Urged on by greed, Balaam tried to act against God's command. But his plans came to nought: a talking ass thwarted his intentions.

Balaam, who is called a prophet because he stood under the special influence of God, was put to shame by a brute animal. Because he let himself be lured away from the right way, all he could undertake was an insane project. And a dumb animal (animals were considered to be symbols of dumbness because they do not speak as humans do) brought him to his senses. The false prophets turn away from the right way, the way of God;

their sphere of activity is restricted to what is humanly possible, and they are driven on by passion. The way of God—his lightsome truth—guarantees us true insight and restrains the passions that of themselves would go to excesses.

DESICCATED SPRINGS (2:17–19)

¹⁷These are waterless springs and mists driven by a storm; for them the nether gloom of darkness has been reserved.

The activity of the false prophets is much ado about nothing. They make great promises, but lead other people to perdition. Springs and clouds give promise of water, of restoration and life. But springs that have dried up in a time of drought, clouds that are driven by winds, only bring disappointment; they do not hold what they promise. False prophets do not lead to the light, but to the " nether gloom of darkness," to estrangement from God, and finally to perdition. To detect false prophets, experience of the kind had by farmers and explorers in judging springs and clouds is necessary. Jesus' dictum: " You will know them by their fruits " (Mt. 7 : 16), has place here.

¹⁸For, uttering loud boasts of folly, they entice with licentious passions of the flesh men who have barely escaped from those who live in error.

The false prophets have a great store of boastful words, finesounding phrases, and concessions to sexuality. With this " bait " they can catch only the inexperienced and immature; they cannot gain people who are knowledgeable and experienced. They are like fishermen who catch fish with bait: behind the enticing appearance of the bait there lurks death.

19They promise them freedom, but they themselves are slaves of corruption; for whatever overcomes a man, to that he is enslaved.

The slogan that the false prophets use is: freedom. Christians know that they are free. But here freedom is twisted to mean libertinism that pays no attention to law and is used as a cover for evil. The freedom that the false prophets proclaim is really a form of slavery, for it leads to sin and damnation. The sinner is not free; he is a slave, for the man who has sinned cannot escape sin by himself (Jn. 8:36). True freedom is not profligacy and the release of instincts, but openness for what is good. Such freedom is a reflection of God's own freedom.

" He who is subject to another, is his slave " was an axiom of the ancient laws of warfare. The conquered becomes the property of the conqueror. Sin wages war against man. If he succumbs, he will be a slave of sin. Man must constantly win his freedom anew in the struggle with sin. Only he who wins is truly free.

The Final State (2 : 20–23)

The false prophets run the risk of relapsing into the heathen ways they once left (2:20). It would be better had they remained heathen, rather than, after their conversion, revert to their former ways (2:21); God condemns such a relapse (2:22).

RELAPSE (2:20)

20For if, after they have escaped the defilements of the world through the knowledge of our Lord and saviour Jesus Christ,

they are again entangled in them and overpowered, the last state
has become worse for them than the first.

Since their baptism, Christians have escaped the grasp of moral
depravity that surrounds them on all sides. What rescued them
was the knowledge of our Lord and saviour Jesus Christ. The
man who has received the gift of this knowledge recognizes
Jesus Christ as Lord and saviour, as God and redeemer; Christ
himself welcomes him into the realm of his salvific power. Paul
has a special expression for this way of life; he calls it " to be in
Christ." This knowledge admits one to the sphere where Jesus'
power is at work, but continued presence there demands continual strengthening in the faith.

Satan and his powers of allurement do not slacken after one
has been baptized. He seeks with all means at his disposal to
lead the convert into moral perdition. The evil spirits entangle
men with their pursuits (2 Tim. 2:4), concerns, and pleasures, to
the end that the convert will lose his knowledge of Christ and
forfeit his freedom. If they succeed, the victim is as helpless as a
sheep caught in brambles.

It is a matter of common experience that perseverance in the
light to which we have been called is no easy matter. The last
state of the man who lapses is worse than the first. This axiom,
taken from human experience, is also applicable to the Christian
life. Jesus used it to warn his followers against relapsing. *Cor-*
ruptio optimi pessima. The Lord provides us with all we need to
lead a true and pure life " in him."

DIRE RESULTS (2:21)

²¹*For it would have been better for them never to have known*

the way of righteousness than after knowing it to turn back from
the holy commandment delivered to them.

The Christian who rejects his faith and returns to a heathen way
of life is in a situation very different from the pagan who (perhaps without guilt) does not know better. Guilt corresponds to
knowledge. " And that servant who knew his master's will, but
did not make ready or act according to his will, shall receive a
severe beating. But he who did not know, and did what deserved
a beating, shall receive a light beating " (Lk. 12:47f.). If Jesus
had not come and had not preached to the Jews, they would not
be guilty of sin; but now they have no excuse (Jn. 15:22). The
experience of the early church made it clear that apostates could
be a greater menace than non-believers. We catch a glimpse of
this in the present epistle.

The faith points out the way of righteousness, the doctrine
that men must follow if they are to stand before God without
blame. The Christian proclamation contains not only truths of
faith but also practical instruction for a life pleasing to God. It
contains both truths to be believed and truths to be lived. The
two are closely linked: a good life is the consequence and application of one's faith.

The way of righteousness is made known by the holy commandment given to Christians. The Lord himself laid down this
commandment and transmitted it to us by the apostles. Because
it is a holy commandment the Christian binds himself to it in
respect and does not dare to change it in any way. He knows he
must live according to this commandment if he intends to serve
God. What commandment would this be if not that of love, of
which Jesus said: " This is my commandment, that you love one
another as I have loved you " (Jn. 15:12).

DISGUSTING BEHAVIOR (2:22)

²²It has happened to them according to the true proverb: The dog turns back to his own vomit, and the sow is washed only to wallow in the mire.

Proverbs are vivid expressions of ancient wisdom garnered from life. The proverb about the dog returning to its vomit comes from the Bible (Prov. 26:11): "Like a dog that returns to his vomit is a fool that repeats his folly." In ancient times the dog and the sow were considered unclean and contemptuous animals. They are mentioned also in the Sermon on the Mount, in the warning not to trust what is holy to men who do not know how to appreciate it (Mt. 7:6). Biblical wisdom draws on both the work of God and the experience of man.

Both proverbs express the disgust of right-thinking men. It is somehow reminiscent of a dog to put back into one's mouth what one has spat out; it is reminiscent of a pig to return to the dirt from which one has washed oneself. The two examples are meant to bring home how hateful it is to return to the life of vice that one has foresworn in baptism.

Christ Will Return (3:1–16)

The false prophets deny the coming of Christ because of its apparent postponement (3:1–4). But its delay is not a proof that it will never take place (3:5–10). God has his own wise reasons for delaying the parousia (3:11–16).

Denial of the Parousia (3:1-4)

Peter writes with pastoral anxiety; he wants to remind his readers of the witnesses who vouch for faith in the parousia (3:1-2). Then he gives the reasons of those who deny the parousia (3:3-4).

PASTORAL RESPONSIBILITY (3:1-2)

¹This is now the second letter that I have written to you, beloved, and in both of them I have aroused your sincere mind by way of reminder; ²that you should remember the predictions of the holy prophets and the commandment of the Lord and saviour through your apostles.

Peter's pastoral zeal urges him on. This is the second epistle now that he has written on the same topic. Whether or not the earlier epistle is the one that we know as 1 Peter remains uncertain. His introductory remark sounds somewhat like an apology: he does not want the letter to be irksome to his readers, and so he addresses them as " beloved." Because they are so important to him, he cannot keep silence about the dangers that threaten them.

He wants to arouse their sincere mind—so that no unclarity or doubt remains, and they can concentrate on the great future event in all sobriety and perspicuity. Paul prayed for the Philippians that their love would grow yet more in knowledge and discernment, so that they would " approve what is excellent, and . . . be pure and blameless for the day of Christ, filled with the fruits of righteousness which come through Jesus Christ, to the glory and praise of God " (Phil. 1:9–11). His overriding pastoral concern is that his readers be prepared for the coming of the Lord. The ministry and apostolate receive their greatest impetus from advent hope. The expectation of the Lord's coming is being dampened by the false prophets, and therefore hope for it must be rekindled in the faithful. This hope is founded on the three greatest authoritative sources of knowledge of the faith: the prophecies of the Old Testament prophets, the commandment of the Lord, and the apostles who delivered the teaching of Christ. The ultimate authority is the Lord and saviour. The prophets looked ahead to his day and the apostles looked back to him.

His commandment (2:21), the new law of Christ, is contained germinally in the Old Testament and is the foundation of apostolic tradition. This " royal " commandment of love is the criterion of faith and life. It is the essence of holy scripture. Scripture is epitomized in it; the two thus appear to the eye of faith as a unity. In this commandment the three authoritative sources of revelation speak: in the Old Testament the prophets, in the gospels the Lord and saviour, in the remaining New Testament writings the apostles. Behind all of them there stands the word of God that in Jesus Christ became flesh (Jn. 1:14). The kingdom thus loses some of its complexity, and the scriptures some of their mysteriousness.

SCOFFERS (3:3–4)

³First of all you must understand this, that scoffers will come in the last days with scoffing, following their own passions . . .

Christians know that the time in which they live is that of the last days. We live in the final aeon of the world. False prophets were foretold for the last days. The ones encountered here are a particular kind, as we saw. They are scoffers with scoffing, wanton persons with their wantonness. Whatever is held to be sacred, they will not take seriously; they have no respect for anything that commands respect. The faithful should not be surprised that such men appear on the scene as teachers in the church. They are a proof that the last days have begun.

The false prophets of the last days live according to their own passions. They reject the commandment of Christ and want to make themselves the law because they fancy themselves perfect. The primal sin of mankind—the rejection of God's holy will—is also their ultimate sin.

⁴*. . . and saying: " Where is the promise of his coming? For ever since the fathers fell asleep, all things have continued as they were from the beginning of creation."*

The scoffers cite two " proofs " against the fulfillment of the parousia promise. The first " proof " runs: " Ever since the fathers fell asleep, all things have continued . . ." The first generation of Christians (the " fathers ") have already died. They had hoped they would witness the second coming of the Lord notwithstanding the many voices that warned against counting on a definite time. Their expectations had not been realized. The false prophets want to conclude: the promise of the coming of Christ in power and glory will never be realized.

Their second " proof " runs: " all things have continued as they were from the beginning of creation." According to the preaching on the last days, at the coming of Christ the world will be convulsed and a new world arise. The cosmic catastrophe and the coming of Christ are interconnected. But experience shows that since its creation the world has not been changed. And if the coming of Christ and the collapse of the present world are interrelated, the first will not take place if the second is not to be expected.

These arguments are certainly understandable, and we would not condemn those who held them. We today can hardly appreciate to the full how deeply the Christians of that time were agitated by this question. But the controversial point of view was a private opinion not in harmony with the entire church. That alone should have made the false prophets more careful in dealing with such an important point of faith. The reasons that the epistle cites strike us as very modern. Today too the same rule of interpretation has to be applied: the correct interpretation of truths of the faith is had only in conjunction with the entire church and its witness to the faith. Private opinion must bow to this criterion.

The Disproof (3:5–10)

The two arguments of the false prophets are now refuted: first the argument based on the contention that the world has not changed since its creation (3:5–7) and then the argument based on the delay of the parousia (3:5–7).

COSMIC CONVULSIONS (3:5–7)

⁵They deliberately ignore this fact, that by the word of God the heavens existed long ago, and an earth formed out of water and by means of water, ⁶through which the world that then existed was deluged with water and perished.

It is not true that the world has not been changed since its creation: the ancient world disappeared in the great deluge (Gen. 7 : 21). The false prophets must have known about this cataclysm. Their objection proves nothing.

Is it then impossible for the world (" heaven and earth ") to come to an end? The same elements that brought it into existence were the same that brought on its ruin: water and the word of God. The ancient world came into existence out of water: " The earth was without form and void, and darkness was upon the face of the deep; and the Spirit of God was moving over the face of the waters " (Gen. 1 : 2). And the ancient world came into existence by means of water: water surrounded it and coursed through it. Water is one of the primal elements of the cosmos. But water alone was not enough. The creative and conserving power of the universe comes from the word of God: " And God said " (Gen. 1). Water and the word of God call the universe into existence; water and the word of God destroy it in the deluge (Gen. 7–8). If the same elements that create the world can also destroy it, what is the basis of the opinion that the world will never end?

The reader who has the same understanding of the world as does the Second Epistle of Peter will be unable to gainsay the cogency of these reflections. The false prophets share the same understanding and the same interpretation of the creation narratives in Genesis and of primeval history in general (Gen. 1–11). If they were of good will, they would have to be convinced.

But the arguments of the epistle do not satisfy the modern reader. According to the epistle, not only men were destroyed in the deluge but the world also. Its interpretation of scripture is the same as that of late Judaism. In the Book of Henoch we read: " Then I saw in a vision the heavens coming apart, shrinking away and falling to the earth. And when it fell to earth I saw the earth disappear into an abyss . . . then a word came from my mouth and I raised my voice and screamed: 'The earth is destroyed!' " (Henoch 83 : 3–5). The Second Epistle of Peter accepts this report because it intends to argue with the false prophets who defend the same interpretation. We know today that this explanation of the deluge is quite impossible; it was a product of its time. Our times must find a new understanding that corresponds to the modern understanding of the world and does not jeopardize the religious truth proclaimed in the texts.

The same applies to the interpretation of the origin of the world. According to the epistle, the world originated from, and by means of, water and the word of God. It puts the emphasis, of course, on the word of God. But when it attributes a special role to water and considers it the primal element of the world, it thinks in the concepts and terms of its own particular era.

When all is said and done, the essential content of the text is something of permanent validity: the world is something perishable. The world is dependent on the will (word) of God. How then can it not perish? He who has called it into existence by his will can also alter it later and destroy it. All created being rests in his hands and is dependent on his will. But God does not act arbitrarily; he acts in accord with his unfathomable plan that is ordained only to glory and life.

⁷But by the same word the heavens and earth that now exist have been stored up for fire, being kept until the day of judgment and destruction of ungodly men.

Just as the ancient world before the deluge was kept in existence for the decree of destruction, so too the present world (" the heavens and earth ") is being kept for its day of judgment and destruction. The second judgment will take place just as surely as did the first: the same divine word is present and operative in both situations. Only the means of destruction differ—and that is a minor factor. In the first instance it was water, in the second it will be fire.

There is little here of the consoling aspect of the second coming of Christ that was of itself the more important aspect: the gathering of believers, the establishment of God's kingdom, the downthrow of all enemies, the victory over death. The reason may be that the epistle had to argue with false prophets who led an unbridled life precisely because of their disbelief in a final judgment. The one-sided view of the parousia given by the epistle does not then represent the church's whole attitude as such to the parousia. The epistle should be judged from the particular aspect of the parousia it sought to defend. Thus the coming of Christ is portrayed as something to be awaited more with fear than with joy and desire.

The Delay of the Parousia (3:8–10)

The Second Epistle of Peter teaches that the delay of the parousia is part of God's plan. It refers to three principles that show this: God's measure of time is different from ours (3:8); God lets himself be moved by mercy (3:9); the period of waiting must not be used frivolously (3:10).

8*But do not ignore this one fact, beloved, that with the Lord one day is as a thousand years, and a thousand years as one day.*

The false prophets think in terms of short periods of time. They measure time in human terms. But God measures it with a divine measure. The psalmist has said: " For God, a thousand years are as one day " (Ps. 90:4). The proclamation of the parousia speaks of the proximity of Jesus' coming. If this proximity is measured in divine terms, it will not be surprising that the parousia is long in coming. Is this " divine measure " only applicable to the time of Christ's coming? Is it not rather that this event escapes all human thought and expression? How are we at all to imagine and picture this last and greatest salvation event? Human powers must here admit their inadequacy. Revelation can express the divine only in human terms. It speaks to men of things that are beyond the human.

⁹The Lord is not slow about his promise as some count slowness, but is forbearing towards you, not wishing that any should perish, but that all should reach repentance.

" Some," namely the false prophets, are talking about the slowness of the parousia to materialize. The word " some " is an indication that the author considers them in the wrong. But also those who expect the parousia in the immediate future are wrong. Human prejudices interfere with a correct understanding of revelation.

If the parousia is slow in coming, it is not a sign that God has gone back on his promise, but that he has forbearance. God does not wish that anyone should perish. God wills to save those members of the community who are in danger of perdition. He wills to give all men the time they need to come to a recognition of the truth and to turn away from their error. The text is an invitation, a summons to conversion. God wills that all men be saved and that no one perish. His will for salvation takes paths that are often difficult for men to understand. But it remains true: " The Lord [is] a God merciful and gracious, slow to anger, and abounding in steadfast love and faithfulness " (Ex. 34 : 6).

¹⁰But the day of the Lord will come like a thief, and then the heavens will pass away with a loud noise, and the elements will be dissolved with fire, and the earth and the works that are upon it will be burned up.

The day of the Lord, coincident with the parousia, has not yet come. Some Christians take it as a proof that the Lord will never come. At one time they believed in the coming of the Lord, but they no longer do so. For their benefit, the epistle refers to the teaching of Jesus that the end will come suddenly and unexpectedly. The Son of man will come when no one expects him. Jesus himself had used the simile of the thief in the night in this context. Peter takes up the simile; we must keep ourselves in readiness, as if we were on the lookout for something.

The day of the Lord will bring with it the end of the world. The destruction will be total. The universe is here divided into three sectors: the heavens (the firmament with everything that pertains to it), the elements (the visible celestial bodies: the sun, moon, and stars), and the earth with the material works of civilization and culture. The cataclysm is described in three different phrases, but all three relate to the whole universe. The universe will pass away with a horrific noise, fire will devastate it, and it will disappear.

The objections of the false prophets have been answered. And thus no one has grounds for erring about the traditional doctrine. The last things will take place. If they have not done so as yet, it is due to God's mercy.

The Last Days and the Moral Life (3 : 11–16)

Having dealt with the *truth* of the last days, it is now time for an application to the moral life. The first part of admonition bears reference to the fact that the present world will be destroyed and a new one arise (3:11–14). The second part refers to the " extension " of time before the coming of the Lord (3:15–16).

THE CHANGE OF THE WORLD
AND THE CONDUCT OF MEN (3:11–14)

[11]*Since all these things are thus to be dissolved, what sort of persons ought you to be in lives of holiness and godliness, . . .*

With the last days, judgment and destruction will occur. Those who fear God will be saved, as the deluge and the destruction of the sinful cities have shown (2:4ff.). This view of the final times is meant to spur us on to a holy and pious way of life. We are on our way to judgment; the all-important decision in our regard is imminent. The possibility of rejecting God, or of making up one's mind too late, is a real possibility (Mt. 22:14). On the day of the Lord we must be without blame (1 Cor. 1:8); we must live according to our conscience so that we can meet Christ in all purity and sinlessness (Phil. 1:10). We must make it our concern to keep our hearts " unblamable in holiness before our God and Father, at the coming of our Lord Jesus with all his saints " (1 Thess. 3:13).

[12]*. . . waiting for and hastening the coming of the day of God, because of which the heavens will be kindled and dissolved, and the elements will melt with fire!*

The coming of the day of God and the beginning of the last
times should not frighten the faithful but awaken in them hope
and joyous expectations. Jesus spoke of the last judgment in the
images of a marriage celebration and a festive banquet. The
primitive community viewed the last days with jubilation. In
the liturgy the community utters the ardent wish: " Maranatha
—come, Lord!" As much as we love this world and enjoy its
beauty, how much more marvelous will be living in happiness
in another yet more radiant world, without tears and pain, without the prospect of death, and especially being " in Christ."

By their holiness of life the faithful hasten the coming of the
day of God. In penance sins are atoned for and " times of re-
freshing " come, and God will send his appointed Christ. The
sins of believers delay the coming of the day of God, because God
has forbearance. The parousia is delayed because the people of
God is not yet holy enough!

The powerful and majestic presence of the glorious day of God
is the reason for the destruction of the world by fire. The ultimate meaning of the dissolution of the world is not simply its
destruction. The glow of the world aflame is, as it were, the
light in which the glory of the day of God is revealed. So too in
the gospel narratives concerning the last times, the destruction of
the old cosmos is, so to say, the background for the glorious
appearance of the Son of man (Mt. 24:29–31). Everything is
ordered to the plenary revelation of God's glory in Jesus Christ
and to the salvation of man.

[13]*But according to his promise, we wait for new heavens and a
new earth in which righteousness dwells.*

New heavens and a new earth are the expectation of those who
cherish hope for the last days. The key word in the promises

regarding the last days is " new." He who attains these promises will drink the new wine of the celestial banquet (Mk. 14:25), will be given a new name (Rev. 2:17), will sing a new anthem (Rev. 5:9), will dwell in the new Jerusalem (Rev. 21:2). This " new " is an indication of the expectation that everything will be other than it presently is—that the incomprehensibility of the divine comprehends everything.

Righteousness dwells in the new earth. The will of God will be done there without exception (Mt. 6:10). Nothing unholy can gain admittance there. The " description " of the new world does not sound like an earthly paradise; the essential thing is the glory of God in everything and everyone.

[14]*Therefore, beloved, since you wait for these, be zealous to be found by him without spot or blemish, and at peace.*

The word "beloved" makes the sentence sound like an entreaty: be righteous—that is, without spot or blemish. Just as the sacrificial animal had to be faultless or it would not be offered to God, so Christians must be presented blameless to God at the end of world history. We must keep our minds fastened on this end event and apply ourselves to the daily struggle. It is a superlative goal that draws us on, through every trouble and affliction.

Even now we should be in peace, in the " state of salvation " (1:2), in grace. The God of peace wills to sanctify us without stint; to make our spirit, soul, and body perfect and blameless. From him come the lofty gifts that we will more and more experience according as we allow him to penetrate our lives more and more. The man who keeps a definite and exalted goal in mind and keeps his passions in check will taste something of this peace of God.

Once again the final judgment is mentioned. Those who intend to have a place in the new world must be found holy. The key word of the whole epistle appears again (1 : 10. 15; 3 : 14): " zeal " in striving for righteousness grounded on the grace and peace given by God. Indefatigable zeal will find entrance into the new world.

MAKING USE OF THE TIME (3 :15–16)

[15a]*And count the forbearance of our Lord as salvation.*

In his forbearance Jesus the Lord makes available to us the time remaining until the final end. This time must be used for conversion and the attainment of salvation. The final days will be preceded by troubled times, the " birth pains " of the messianic era: trials, earthly needs, natural catastrophes, persecution, and opposition. By God's mercy these afflictions can be used to our salvation, because they can lead every new generation to conversion.

[15b]*So also our beloved brother Paul wrote to you according to the wisdom given him,* [16a]*speaking of this as he does in all his letters.*

Paul's epistles confirm what Peter is saying. The two of them are the pillars of the church and the princes of the apostles. Paul is the beloved brother because he is a co-apostle. God gave him special wisdom. His authority does not rest on human grounds but on the gift of God. In any question touching on a crucial issue of the faith his wisdom is to be consulted. On this matter of the Christian's preparation for the last days he had laid down some fundamental guidelines. The different writings of the New Testament complement and clarify one another. All of them must be studied in order to have the fullest possible understanding of revelation.

[16b]*There are some things in them hard to understand, which the ignorant and unstable twist to their own destruction, as they do the other scriptures.*

The false prophets misuse the scriptures. They interpret them arbitrarily and use them to confuse those who are unlearned and unstable in the teaching of tradition (1:21). The Pauline epistles seem to have been the most misused. This is no surprise, for they contain " some things hard to understand." Paul writes on Christian freedom (Gal. 4:13), spiritual men (1 Cor. 3:1), the relationship between body and spirit (Gal. 4:13ff.), and the last days (1 Cor. 15:50. 53f.; 2 Thess. 2:2); what he writes is easily misunderstood and was gleefully seized on by the false prophets. They could use Paul, or so they thought, to give their own teaching the appearance of apostolic authority. It is possible too that they wanted to play Peter against Paul (1 Cor. 1:12). The Pauline writings are a treasure-trove of Christian wisdom, cautions, theological knowledge, and knowledge of salvation history—but he is not easy to understand, as we ourselves are constantly aware.

The scriptures are not to be interpreted arbitrarily, but only according to the Spirit of God who inspired them (1:20f.). To this principle a second can be added: they must be interpreted in accord with the truth held traditionally in the church, in accord with what the church has taught and teaches. He who reads the scriptures in the spirit of the church and knows well the teaching of faith has the wherewithal to grasp their true meaning. And still one must always be ready to hear the scriptures anew, to be open and allow oneself to be taught—especially when it is not a question of something customary. What Peter teaches and Paul writes in his epistles is " profitable for teaching, for reproof, for correction, and for training in righteousness, that the man of God may be complete, equipped for every good work " (2 Tim. 3 : 16).

The warning attached to the teaching on the parousia ends with the words: " to their own destruction." The false prophets misinterpret the scriptures or make little of them. Eternal perdition faces them. Only he who denies himself and accepts the word of God as it is and as the apostles and the church have " delivered " it will find salvation. Often only a shade of difference, a small shift of meaning, a one-sided emphasis—and the reader has turned away from the whole Bible. Our way is sure if we set aside our own obstinacy and curiosity, and allow ourselves to be led by the Holy Spirit and the teaching authority of the church.

THE CLOSE OF THE LETTER
(3:17-18)

THE CLOSE OF THE LETTER (3:17-18)

A warning not to let oneself be led astray (3:17), a wish for growth in the Christian life (3:18a), and a doxology (3:18b) bring the epistle to a close.

[17]*You therefore, beloved, knowing this beforehand, beware lest you be carried away with the error of lawless men and lose your own stability.*

At the most important parts of the epistle, the faithful are addressed as " beloved " (3:1. 8. 14. 17). The Christian lives in love: in the love of God, of the apostle, and of his fellow Christians. Love is the only atmosphere in which the Christian can maintain and develop his life.

The epistle assures that the faithful know beforehand what dangers are posed by the false prophets. A danger known in advance loses much of its power. What the false prophets are doing is exposed as deception and treachery. They do not come as messengers of God; they are deceivers who care nothing about the will of God. But their power to sunder the community is lessened because they have been exposed. The teaching of the church explained by a true pastor offers genuine protection in the struggle against error. The man who thinks himself beyond error must also take care, for he too can lose his footing. " Let anyone who thinks that he stands take heed lest he fall " (1 Cor. 10:12).

^{18a}*But grow in the grace and knowledge of our Lord and saviour Jesus Christ.*

Both blessing and warning find a place in this epistle. The wish of verse 2 is repeated. Grace and knowledge come from Christ. Both gifts are to increase and grow. All life is change and growth. We will survive all trials if we do not cease our efforts for betterment. God is always present to us and gives us his gifts; we too must always be " underway," active, zealous—with our glorious end always in view.

^{18b}*To him be the glory both now and to the day of eternity. Amen.*

A solemn expression of praise (doxology) ends the epistle. It is addressed to our Lord and saviour Jesus Christ. Such doxologies are usually addressed to God (Jude 25). A living faith in the divinity of Jesus fills this entire epistle; it had given him the highest titles. This robust faith easily passes into prayer. The doxology does not express a wish, but simply states in laudatory acknowledgment what it believes: the fullness of divine glory resides in Christ.

This glory is his now and will be his on the day of his coming —it is his for all eternity. The day that dawns on his mighty coming will never end. " Jesus Christ is the same yesterday and today and for ever " (Heb. 13:8).